BOOK 1

CAMBRIDGE INTRODUCTION
TO THE HISTORY OF MANKIND

*Kochanym Buddzie i Kropee
od Su i Ko
Gwiardu 1972*

men become civilized

Trevor Cairns

art editors Banks and Miles

CAMBRIDGE, AT THE UNIVERSITY
PRESS, 1969

Illustrations for this volume
have been specially drawn by
Anne Micke
Alan Rhodes
Peter Taylor
Maurice Wilson

Published by the Syndics of the Cambridge University Press
Bentley House, 200 Euston Road, London NW1.

American Branch: 32 East 57th Street, New York, N.Y. 10022

© Cambridge University Press 1969

Library of Congress Catalogue Card Number:
Standard Book Number:
521 07226 3 School

Thanks are due to the following for permission to reproduce
plates in this book:

p10 British Museum (Natural History); p16 Instituto de
Espana en Londres; pp18, 20 Australian News and
Information Bureau; p20 Mansell Collection; p23 Swedish
Tourist Traffic Association, Israel Government Tourist
Office, Royal Geographical Society; pp26, 27 Jericho
Excavation Fund; pp32, 42, 43, 45, 46, 47, 63, 66, 87 British
Museum; pp33, 66 Metropolitan Museum of Art, New
York; pp35, 37 Roger Wood; p44 Louvre; pp46, 52, 63, 74
Edwin Smith; p52 Ecole Française d'Athenes; pp63, 75
Radio Times–Hulton Picture Library; p69 British Museum
(Science); p73 Banks and Miles; p89 Mansell–Brogi–
Giraudon; p91 India Office Library.

TYPE-SET BY HAZELL, WATSON AND VINEY
PRINTED AND BOUND IN GREAT BRITAIN
BY JARROLD AND SONS LTD, NORWICH

contents

This chart spans 600 million years.
It shows that man is a very recent arrival.
Here are some of the common groups of animals
and their fossil forms. You can see
most of them in the natural history part
of a museum.

Dimetrodo

Amphibian

Endothiod

Holoptychius   Cornuboniscus   Pleuracar

Ammonite

Sea Lily

Lingulella

Harknessella

Pentamerus

Spirifer

Productus

Horridonia

Sponge

Graptolite

Coral

Coral

Coral

time of arrival in million years past   4600   600   500   440   400   350   270

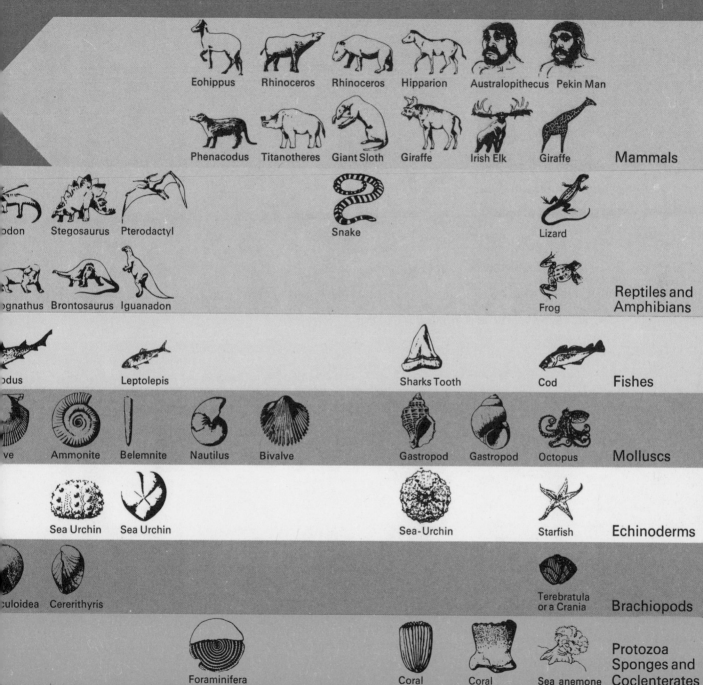

Eohippus · Rhinoceros · Rhinoceros · Hipparion · Australopithecus · Pekin Man

Phenacodus · Titanotheres · Giant Sloth · Giraffe · Irish Elk · Giraffe

Mammals

...odon · Stegosaurus · Pterodactyl · Snake · Lizard

...ognathus · Brontosaurus · Iguanadon · Frog

Reptiles and Amphibians

...odus · Leptolepis · Sharks Tooth · Cod

Fishes

...ve · Ammonite · Belemnite · Nautilus · Bivalve · Gastropod · Gastropod · Octopus

Molluscs

Sea Urchin · Sea Urchin · Sea-Urchin · Starfish

Echinoderms

...culoidea · Cererithyris · Terebratula or a Crania

Brachiopods

Foraminifera · Coral · Coral · Sea anemone

Protozoa Sponges and Coelenterates

180   135   70   40   25   11   1   1/4

Why learn history?

Because history

is about people

It is about all sorts of people,

    great and small, good and bad.

It tells you how people have behaved

    in all sorts of times and places ;

    what they have made and what they have

    destroyed ; how they have worked together

    and how they have fought.

Anything that people have ever done is History.

1. BEFORE CIVILIZATION

The first people

How do you tell the difference between people and animals?

This may seem a silly question now, but if we want to know how people first began it is a very important question. For millions of years there were no men and women in the world. In fact, there were no living things at all.

At first, the world was just a huge desert. There was nothing but rock and water and mud.

Then came the plants, and the only living things were ferns, trees, grasses. Many of these grew in tropical swamps which vanished millions of years ago. Some of the trees became buried, and have gradually been turned into coal.

While all this was very slowly happening, some sort of animal life seems to have begun in the water. Things rather like frog-spawn and jellyfish came, and then things with shells. Millions of years slowly passed, and new living things came.

There were the first fishes.

Then some of these began to live partly on the land, as well as in the water. Such creatures are called amphibians.

Next came reptiles which lived mostly on land, beasts which could not breathe under water. They were of all shapes and sizes, and they had all sorts of habits. Some ate leaves, and others ate flesh. Some had such big bodies that they seem to have spent most of their time standing in lakes, to take part of the weight off their legs. Others were able to fly. These reptiles, which we call dinosaurs, sometimes grew to a size of thirty, forty or even eighty feet. They died out millions of years ago.

Birds and warm-blooded animals, more like those which we know today, came instead of the dinosaurs.

Last of all came people.

Animal life seems to have begun in the water.
Early forms of life survive to this day in ponds, streams and seas.

Next came reptiles. Very many died out, including tyrannosaurus, which ate flesh ; triceratops, which ate plants ; and the flying pterandon.

Warm-blooded animals came. Though the sabre-tooth and mastodon no longer exist, their relatives are still doing well.

We know all this because scientists called geologists have studied the different rocks and earth. They can tell how one kind of earth or rock was laid on another, how all these layers were sometimes twisted and jumbled up by earthquakes or volcanoes, and how they were sometimes worn away by wind and rain, or scraped and ground by ice. You can learn about this in Geography.

In the rocks the geologists sometimes find the bones of the creatures which lived very long ago – so long ago that the bones have turned to stone, and more stone has formed round them. Such bones are called fossils. This picture shows you a fossil which is still in the rock.

Geologists can make a rough guess at how many millions of years it has taken the rock to form. That tells us roughly how many millions of years ago those fossil bones belonged to a live animal, a dinosaur perhaps.

By studying the bones themselves, other scientists can tell us how the animal's body worked.

A fossil icthyosaurus, perhaps as much as 190 million years old, found embedded in limestone at Street, Somerset.

You may be wondering why we should spend time on rocks and fossils. They are not people, and History is about people. There are two good reasons.

First, you can see now how very old the world was before the earliest people came. Look at the chart on pages 4 and 5 and you will see that, compared with the earth and the plants and the animals, people have only just arrived in the world.

Second, we have to use the same methods of finding out about the first people as we use to find out about the first animals.

The 'tree of life' shows how different forms of life have branched out at different times. Some branches have withered, others have flourished and grown new shoots. It has all happened very gradually, over hundreds of millions of years.

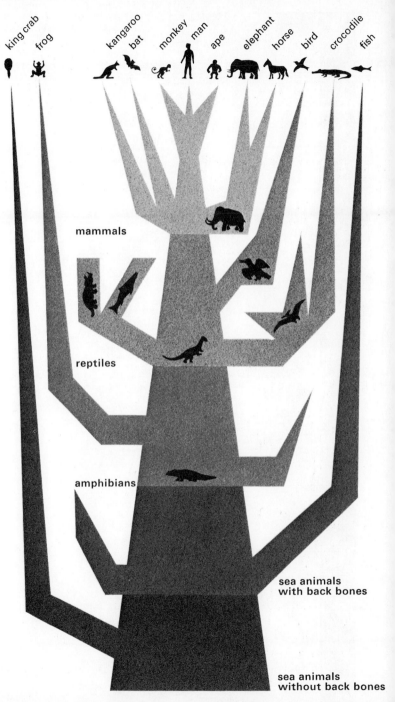

king crab   frog   kangaroo   bat   monkey   man   ape   elephant   horse   bird   crocodile   fish

mammals

reptiles

amphibians

sea animals
with back bones

sea animals
without back bones

Now we can return to the question we started with. How can you tell the difference between people and animals? On page 12 are some pictures of what some of the earliest people probably looked like. Which of them, do you think, is like you? Which of them is near enough to you to be called a human being?

Telling the difference between people and animals can sometimes be very difficult because in some ways man is an animal. A human body, for example, very often works in the same way as an animal's body. Some animals look and behave like people in many ways, others do not seem to be like people at all. You will probably learn in Science how all living things are related, about how one sort of plant or animal seems to have descended from another. This is a big and difficult subject, and it is not really part of History. But it is interesting, and here is a diagram, a sort of 'Family Tree', which will show you how scientists think that all living things are related.

Even if man is related to animals, though, there are several differences between even the most animal-like men and the most man-like animals. You will see this if you try to make a list of the differences between even primitive men on the one side and clever apes on the other. You could begin such a list now, and go on adding to it. There are the physical differences, of course. There are the differences in the sort of foods they eat, how they eat them and how they get them. There are differences in the sort of work they do, how they share it out, the tools they use or make to help them. There are differences in how they live together, in their families, in their homes, in the way they tell each other things and the sort of things they are able to tell. There are differences in what they do when they are not busy on the jobs they must do in order to stay alive. There are differences in what they can learn and make.

Even the very earliest people were very different from any other living things.

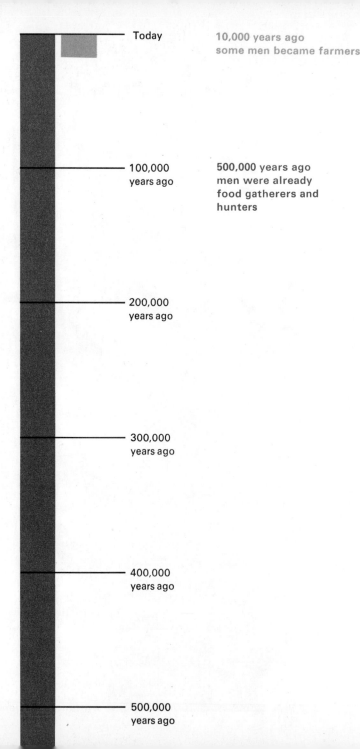

Today

10,000 years ago
some men became farmers

100,000
years ago

500,000 years ago
men were already
food gatherers and
hunters

200,000
years ago

300,000
years ago

400,000
years ago

500,000
years ago

Gathering food and hunting

When you want to eat, the obvious thing to do is what an animal would do; go and get it. If there are no shops, no farms, no gardens, no tools, no weapons you will just have to take what you can find. Sometimes you may eat fruit, berries, seeds, nuts, roots. Sometimes you may be able to kill and eat some animal; all sorts of animals will do, including birds, fish, reptiles and grubs. If you are lucky and clever you will find enough to stay alive.

That is how everybody had to live until quite a short time ago, comparatively. Look at this date-line, and you will see that for most of the time when there have been people in the world, the people have been living like that. The first men may have lived half a million years ago, or perhaps far longer. Even the simplest farming did not begin until about ten thousand years ago. Ten thousand years may seem a long time, but not when you compare it with half a million.

During all that time, between half a million years ago and ten thousand years ago, when people had to live by gathering or hunting food, they simply had to do better than the animals, or die. Many of the animals were faster, stronger, better armed with teeth and claws than any man. Man's advantage was his brain.

One of the most important things that men could learn to do was to work together, to share out their jobs so that the work

1 Australopithecus, who first appeared about 1,000,000 years ago.

2 Pithecanthropus, Pekin or Java Man, lived from approximately 550,000–200,000 years ago.

3 Neanderthal Man is thought to have died out about 40,000 years ago.

4 Magdelanian Man, who existed up to approximately 12,000 years ago.

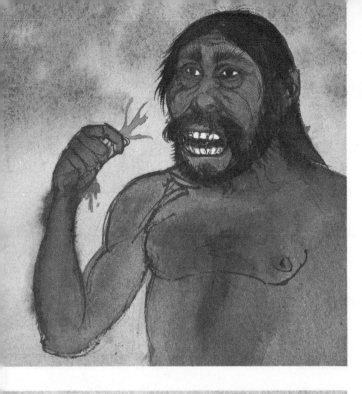

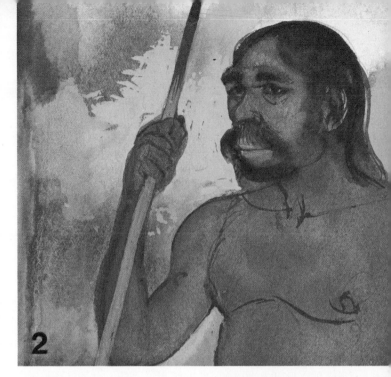

could be done better. Animals cannot talk, but men can. The early hunters could tell their friends or families what they had found out, or make plans to help each other to kill big animals. Work could be shared out between men and women, too. While the men hunted for meat, the women would be busy looking after the children or gathering food from plants.

Probably the groups of people who helped each other like this were families; they would be big families, or tribes. The children would be taught by the older people. When a man or woman discovered something new, he or she would pass it on, so that the discovery would not be lost. The children could first learn from the grown-ups, and then, when they grew up, they could perhaps learn something new for themselves. In this way, every new set of children would have a chance to do a little better than their fathers and mothers. Sometimes, we may guess, they did not take their chance. Sometimes they did, and became a little more skilful than their fathers and had a rather more comfortable life.

One of the most important things that these early people did was something else that animals could not do. They learned how to make tools. When you were looking at the pictures of early people on page 12, you must have seen that some of them were holding a tool or weapon. Here are some pictures of such tools, and diagrams to show how they were made.

We can be sure about these stone tools, because so many of them have been found. Stone does not rot away like wood, bone or leather, which must also have been used widely. The time when nobody in the world had anything better than tools like these is called the Old Stone Age.

People living such a hard and simple life would not leave behind very much for us to find. Their homes, where the women and children would stay while the hunters searched for meat, were only rough shelters. Often they were in the mouths of caves, probably with a rough screen of brushwood or skins to keep out the weather. Sometimes they were just holes in the ground, with skins stretched over sticks laid across the top.

From their tools and homes we can guess something about how the Old Stone Age men lived. We have also found in some places the bones of their dead. These bones, as you have seen, tell us about what these people looked like. They sometimes tell us something more. Sometimes we can see that the dead person was very carefully buried, with tools or ornaments beside the body. It seems that these Stone Age men did

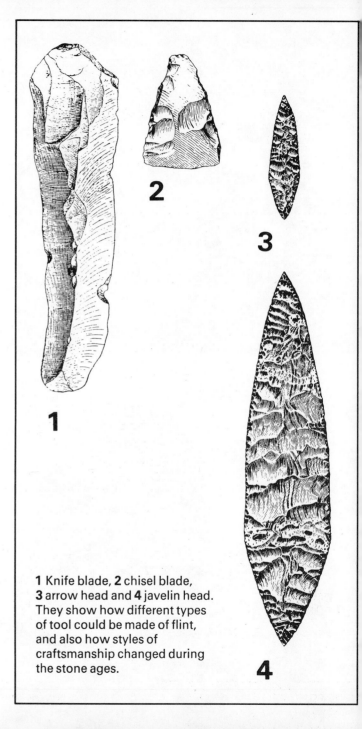

1 Knife blade, **2** chisel blade, **3** arrow head and **4** javelin head. They show how different types of tool could be made of flint, and also how styles of craftsmanship changed during the stone ages.

14

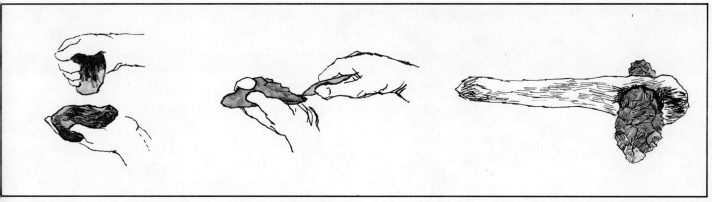

Flaking the flint, the first and most important skill in tool making.

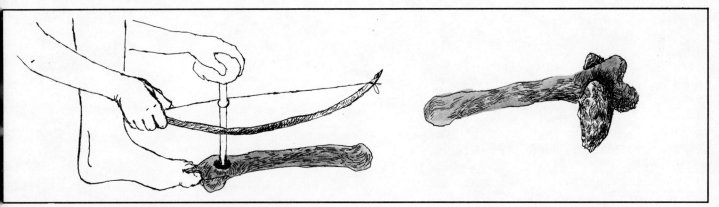

Drilling : a tool is far more use with a good handle.

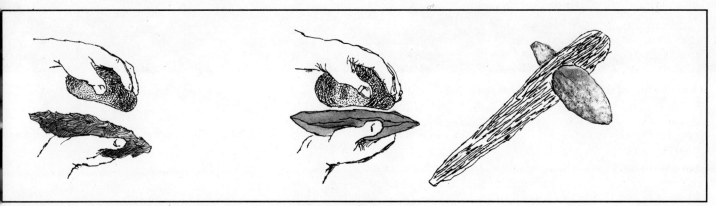

Polishing : a very late development. The smoother the tool, the better it cuts.

A bison, from the caves at Altamira, Spain.

right: Probably a magician, from the Trois Frères caves, France

far right: Hunting scene, from Cueva de los Caballos, Spain

not believe that when a man died he was completely wiped out. These people must have had some sort of religion.

The people who lived in the later part of the Old Stone Age have left behind other things which make us think that they had a religion. Deep in some of their caves, down in the darkness, far from the light of the cave-mouths where people lived, they painted some wonderful pictures. Though the painters lived near the end of the Old Stone Age, when men had been on the earth for hundreds of thousands of years already, they were still living a hard, rough, dangerous life. Yet they were fine artists, as you can see for yourself by looking at these pictures. They were the first great artists in the history of the world. Probably they had other arts, too: music and dancing of some sort. Only the paintings are still there for us to admire.

The pictures are more than decorations. Do you see the spears and arrows sticking in some of the animals? That may be a form of magic. The idea is that by 'killing' the picture the hunter has a better chance of killing the real animal. (Only a few hundred years ago, witches were supposed to melt or stick pins into wax models of people they wished to harm, and we still go on burning Guy Fawkes.) Another sign of the magic, or perhaps the religion, of these people is the horned man. He was probably some sort of 'medicine man', witch doctor or priest.

Some of the words in the last sentence may have given you an idea about another way of discovering how people lived in the Old Stone Age. There are still people in some parts of the world living in Old Stone Age conditions. There are the bushmen of the Kalahari Desert and some of the tribes in the jungles of the Amazon. Until recently most of the Australian aborigines and the people of New Guinea were still living as their forefathers had done, hundreds and thousands of years ago. Until less than a hundred years ago many Red Indian and Eskimo tribes were also Old Stone Age people.

Eskimo fisherman. They are spearing fish which they have trapped in a rough tank.

A hunter in New Guinea.

As these two pictures show, men can live the hunting and food-gathering life of the Old Stone Age in the cold wastes of the Arctic or in equatorial heat. Even in the same country, the climate can change very much over thousands of years. Once it was very warm in Britain, and at other times most of the land was covered by ice.

Of course we can do a tremendous number of things that the Old Stone Age people could not even dream of; but they knew how to live under conditions which would kill most of us. We know this, because we have discovered enough about them to be able to imagine the sort of life they lived.

Beyond that we know nothing. We know neither the name nor the life-story of a single one. We cannot tell what gods they worshipped, what chiefs they followed, what stories they told. We do not know when or how they first found out how to use fire, or tamed dogs to help in hunting. These things we shall probably never know.

We can be fairly sure about one other thing. Our fathers and mothers had fathers and mothers themselves, and so you can look back to grand-parents and great-grand-parents. Some people can trace their families back for hundreds of years, although even they cannot go back very far. But though not one of us knows who they were, we all have ancestors who lived in the Old Stone Age. All of us, whatever the colour of our skin or the language we speak, have the blood of those people in our own veins.

Look again at the chart and pictures on pages 11 and 12. Remember that animals have been here far longer than men, and that men have lived the rough, hard, dangerous life of the Old Stone Age far longer than they have been civilized.

The earliest farmers

Farming was discovered. Sometimes it is said that this was the most important thing that ever happened to mankind.

Once again, we have to admit that we do not know how and when it happened, nor exactly where. The experts who have studied it guess that the story was something like this:

In most Old Stone Age tribes the men did the hunting while the women collected anything that grew near the camp and seemed fit to eat. Sometimes the women could find nothing better than the seeds of some kinds of tall grass. They discovered how to dry the seeds. They tried beating the seeds to get rid of the bits of husk which clung to them. Then they began to grind the seeds between two stones, and to mix the powder they got with water, to form a sort of paste. Can you give the correct names to all these things? As for the grass, you will have guessed what it was: wild corn. The women depended on finding some near their camp, or the next camp.

Then somebody had a brilliant idea. Why not make sure that the corn would be there? Why not plant some of the seeds, on purpose?

Once this happened, everything else followed. People stopped wandering far from the places where the corn grew best. At last they stopped wandering altogether, and built themselves permanent shelters near their fields. The first villages were made. The villagers spent more and more of their time planting corn, breaking up the soil with a digging stick. Also, they learned how to get better crops by choosing the best seed for sowing.

Wild wheat, the ancestor of cultivated wheat.

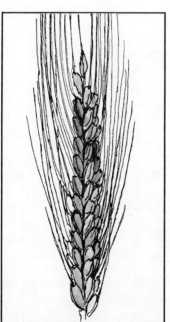

Wheat cultivated by the early farmers. It had more ears.

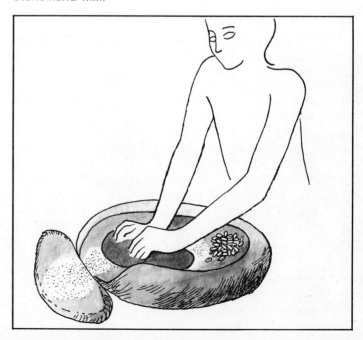

Stone hand-mill.

But what about the hunters and the wild animals? Did they suddenly stop hunting and eating meat? Of course not. Even today, in civilized countries, people still hunt, though it is more for amusement than because they want to eat what they catch. We can eat meat without having to depend on hunters to go out and find it for us. This is something else that was discovered by the earliest farmers.

Once again, we have to guess how it happened. Perhaps tribes of hunters got into the habit of always sticking to the same herds of wild cattle. At first they would follow the herds where they wandered, in something like the way the Red Indians used to follow the great herds of buffalo. Gradually the Stone Age hunters must have begun to guide the herds where they wanted the animals to go, to the pastures which were rich and most easily reached. They would keep the half-wild animals on these pastures, as the cowboys kept their great herds of cattle on the range. At last, some animals would become tame enough to be kept in farms. Then the farmers could control the breeding of the animals, and at last produce the sort of farm animals we know today.

So it became possible for some people to settle down in villages with corn-fields and tame animals, instead of wandering far and wide, looking for food. Now these people could build houses, make furniture and pots and pans. Now they had a little more time to spend on making things, amusing themselves and thinking up new ideas. Some people were just about to become 'civilized', as we now call it.

Where did all this happen? If you look at the page of maps opposite, you will see the home of wild corn and the home of the first animals to be tamed or domesticated. In the same region early civilizations arose. This suggests that it happened in some parts of the Middle East, and archaeologists have found evidence pointing in the same direction. The New Stone Age, as it has been called, may have begun about 10,000 years ago, or 8000 B.C. if we want to write the date in the way historians do. By about 6000 B.C. the farmers who had been using bags, baskets and wooden containers were beginning to make pottery as well. They were living a more settled life, with more belongings than the Old Stone Age people had had. They were gradually making a tremendous discovery. For hundreds of

North American Indians hunting bison; a sketch made in 1841 by an artist who spent a long time with the Indians.

Australians rounding up cattle: a modern photograph.

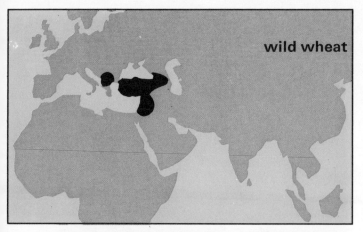

wild wheat

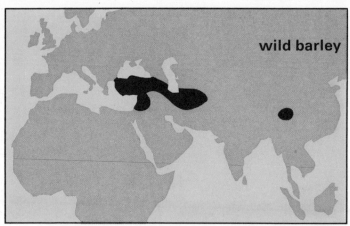

wild barley

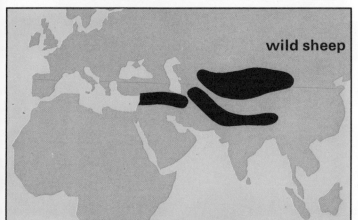

wild sheep

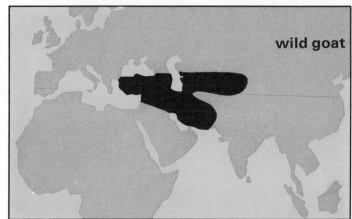

wild goat

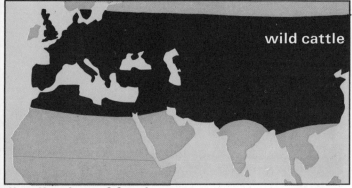

wild cattle

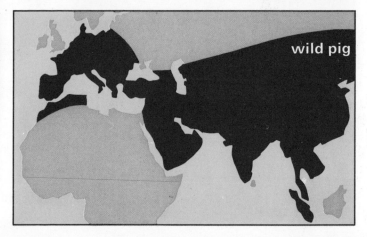

wild pig

**distribution of food
at the start of the new stone age**

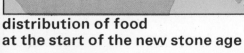

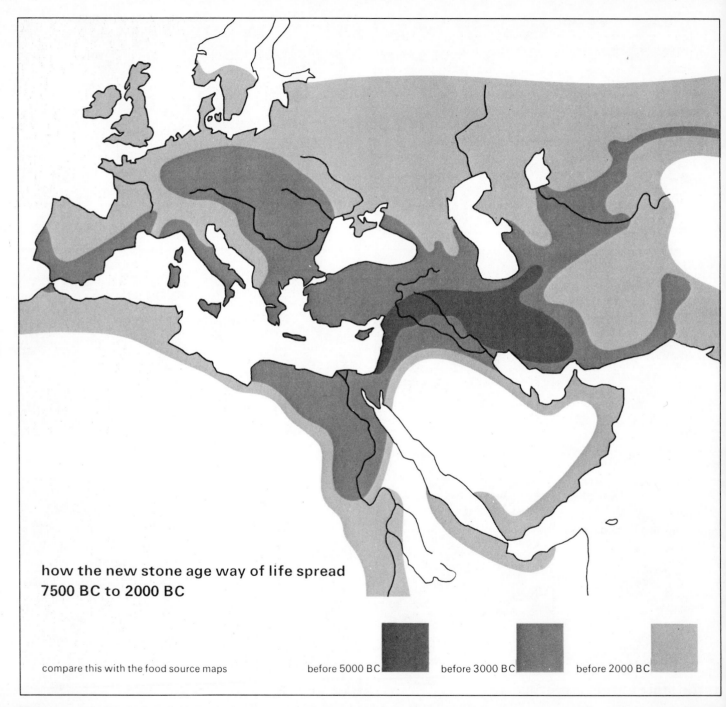

how the new stone age way of life spread
7500 BC to 2000 BC

compare this with the food source maps

before 5000 BC   before 3000 BC   before 2000 BC

thousands of years men had just fitted in with the world as they found it, and had done their best to live on wild animals and plants. These New Stone Age farmers were coming to see that *sometimes men can change their surroundings to suit themselves.*

The new way of life spread slowly. The first New Stone Age people to reach Britain, for example, with their corn, farm animals and pottery, did not arrive until about 3000 B.C. By this time men in the Middle East were founding splendid civilizations. When we compare this change with the hundreds of thousands of years that the Old Stone Age had lasted, it seems very quick. Because of this, and because the change in the way people lived was so big, it is sometimes described as a revolution; 'Neolithic Revolution' is the name sometimes given to the changes which took place in the New Stone Age. Remember, though, that it took thousands of years, and the changes must have been so slow that the people who were alive then would hardly have noticed them. There would not have been much difference between the sort of life that most people knew when they were children and the sort of life they knew when they were old men and women.

It took thousands of years for the farming villages of the New Stone Age to grow, and for these to become the foundations of great civilizations. It was slow, and the men who did the work could have had no idea about the future they were making. Without the discoveries and work of those early farmers, we should all still be living in the Old Stone Age.

Some people never settled down. We have already mentioned, on page 17, some who went on living an Old Stone Age life until very recently. There were others who tamed animals, but did not grow crops. Here are some pictures of such people. They lead the same sort of life, but in very different climates. They all live in lands where it would be hard to grow crops, but where there is just enough pasture for the right sort of animal. So the herdsmen move from pasture to pasture with their flocks and herds. They are wanderers, or nomads, like the Old Stone Age hunters, but they live a pastoral instead of a hunting life.

Nomadic tribes like these are usually tough and poor. Often they are expert robbers and fighters. Later you may hear much about some of these tribes, and what happened when they came against people who had settled down to enjoy a civilized life.

Lapps.

Mongol women.

Bedouin Arab.

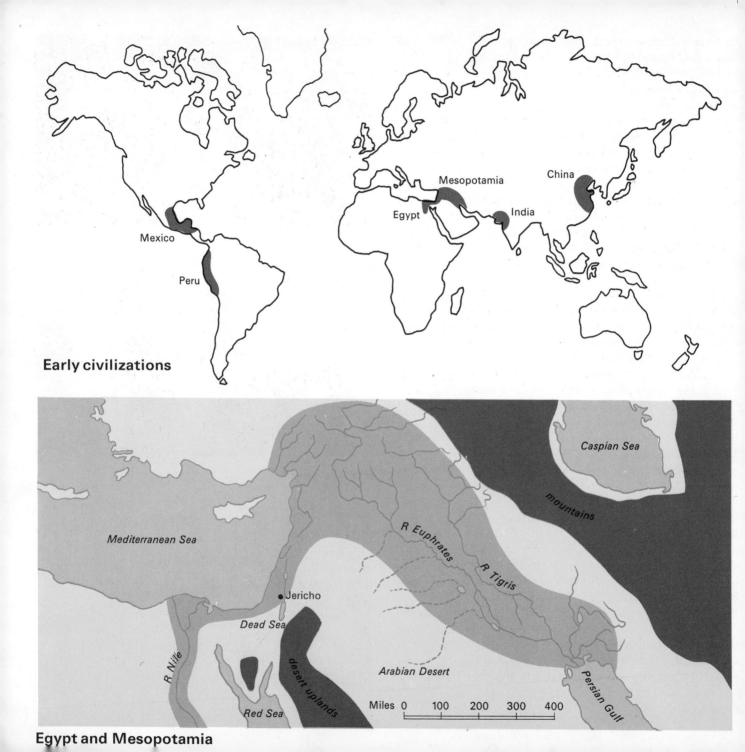

Early civilizations

Mexico

Peru

Egypt

Mesopotamia

India

China

Egypt and Mesopotamia

Caspian Sea

mountains

Mediterranean Sea

R Euphrates

R Tigris

Jericho

Dead Sea

R Nile

Arabian Desert

Persian Gulf

desert uplands

Red Sea

Miles 0   100   200   300   400

2. THE EARLIEST CIVILIZATIONS

Civilization

Do you think that you and the people you know are civilized? Most of us think that we are. Do you know of any people who are not civilized? What do you think the difference is? Not very long ago we were thinking about the differences between people and animals. Now, can you tell the differences between civilized people and uncivilized people?

It is a very difficult question to answer. We all think that we know, but it turns out not to be so easy when we try to put it into words.

One old way of judging was by asking if the people had cities to live in. People in cities were supposed to be civilized. They had learnt to live in peace together, by making and obeying laws. They had learnt to combine in order to protect each other from enemies and criminals. They built walls, houses, temples and palaces. Living and working together, they were able to invent many things, to make and to trade many sorts of goods.

Before they could begin to do all this, these people had to have the right conditions. If people are so poor and have to work so hard to keep themselves alive that they never have any time to spare, they are not likely to think of building cities and inventing things.

On the opposite page you see two maps. The map of the world shows the places where, as far as we can tell, civilizations started without any help from outside. Now you need to know some Geography, and to look at your atlas. Do you notice how the places are arranged? All but one are practically on the same latitude. Think about the climate. And what about the fertility of the land, and the rivers? What about the lands surrounding the places marked on the map; do you see how often they are barren deserts or mountains?

Of the civilizations marked on the map of the world, those in America (Mexico and Peru) were wiped out by their conquerors 400 years ago. In the Far East, India and China have been the homes of great civilizations ever since civilization began there, three or four thousand years ago. In the Middle East (Egypt and Mesopotamia) were the civilizations which seem to have given most to the people of Europe. Partly because our own civilization begins there, partly because they seem to be the oldest homes of civilization in the world, and partly because more is at present known about them than about the other early civilizations, we had better begin by taking a closer look at the Middle East.

The lower map is a close-up of the Middle East. You can see at a glance why people would prefer to live in some places rather than others in this area.

These are lands full of the remains of ancient cities, many of them under huge mounds of earth or sand. Often cities have been built and rebuilt on the same site, so that under the top layer of ruins there are many others, like an enormous sandwich cake. Many of these great mounds of buried, ruined cities have never been properly explored; there may be many buried cities which have not even been found yet.

Of all these old lost cities, which is the oldest? At present, experts think that Jericho may be the oldest real city that has been found. You can see enough from the pictures on pages 28 and 29 to realize how different life in Jericho about 6000 B.C. was from life in the Old Stone Age. Whether or not you can call these people civilized is a question that is hard to answer, that you may want to argue about.

The archaeologists who explored Jericho found some surprising things. There were the plaster heads, for example – like the one opposite. They were well made and painted, and were found under the floors of some of the houses. Inside each plaster head is a human skull. Why they were put there is a mystery. Perhaps it had something to do with religion or magic, but we can only guess.

Another surprise was that these early citizens of Jericho had no pottery. They knew how to farm well and build a city with big walls and comfortable houses before they knew how to make even the simplest pots.

Archaeologists are still trying to find out where and when some of the important discoveries were made. Pottery is one. Metal is another; we do not yet know where and when men discovered how to make copper tools, though it must have been in a place where copper ore was found. The wheel is another. The earliest writing is another.

When discoveries like these were made there would be new jobs. Men would become skilled craftsmen. There would then have to be the exchanging of goods: that is, trade.

The great and famous civilizations of the river valleys, like the Egyptian civilization in the valley of the Nile, used all these discoveries. When you learn about what these civilizations were like you may notice that some of their greatest works would have been impossible without a lot of other things which had happened before. People like the Egyptians did not start from scratch.

Look again at the map of the Middle East on page 24. You will see that Jericho is not in one of the great river valleys. Jericho is the most famous, but there are other places outside the great river valleys where archaeologists are trying to find out how far New Stone Age farmers had already gone before the great civilizations were founded. It may be that it was only when men were already skilled farmers and craftsmen, when they had already learned to live together in villages and even in towns or cities, that they were able to use the rich but difficult land in the river valleys.

26

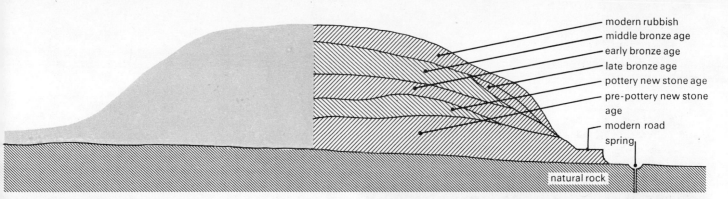

modern rubbish
middle bronze age
early bronze age
late bronze age
pottery new stone age
pre-pottery new stone age
modern road
spring
natural rock

The Jericho mound : it was already about 45 feet high before the inhabitants began to use pottery.

A plaster head found at Jericho

The town walls of Jericho, dating from the pre-pottery new stone age, nearly 9,000 years ago.

Everyday life in Jericho

Jericho is important, not only because it is one of the very oldest towns to have been discovered so far, but especially because men lived there continuously for a very long time. The painting opposite tries to show what life was like when the third set of town walls was still in use. The people pasture their herds at the oasis, like nomads, but crops are being cultivated there too. Later generations produced pottery of varied types for various purposes, as you can see here, and eventually learned how to make such things as the bronze pin.

The Egyptians

Hundreds of miles long and only two or three miles wide – that is Egypt. As you saw, most of the early civilizations had something to do with rivers, but none so obviously as Egypt.

The valley of the Nile is surrounded by vast deserts, but into this narrow valley the river brings, as it floods every year, water and rich mud. Where it reaches the sea, the river Nile has spread a broad delta, partly swamp and partly good fertile soil. With the Nile beside them and the sun above, the Egyptians were able to make one of the first and greatest civilizations.

So as to make the most of their water, the Egyptians learned how to irrigate. They dug channels to carry the water to and through their fields. They also used machines to lift water from the river to the fields; some of these machines were simple cranes, but eventually elaborate machines for screwing the water up from the river were invented.

Farming was only the beginning. To farm well, the Egyptians had to know the seasons of the year exactly, especially because it was important to know when the Nile was due to flood. This meant that they had to study the sun and the stars, and they invented a calendar with 365 days in the year.

They had to be able to count, of course, but they became so good at measuring and counting that they were able to build great Pyramids. (If you think that this is easy, try to build a model with little blocks of wood, and then imagine having to do it on an enormous scale, in stone.) The base of the biggest Pyramid is $755\frac{1}{2}$ feet square, according to the best modern measurements; the Egyptian builders were so exact that the difference between the longest side and the shortest side is less than eight inches. The corners are almost exact right angles, and the building stands very nearly north–south, east–west. The Egyptians did all this without the instruments that modern surveyors use, but they managed to be very accurate.

The work that went into the Great Pyramid was enormous. Experts think that about 2,300,000 blocks of stone were used; the average weight was about two and a half tons, and the biggest block would weigh about fifteen tons. Nobody knows how long it took to build, nor how many men worked on it. Herodotus the Greek, who wrote more than 2,000 years ago, was told by Egyptians that 100,000 men laboured twenty years on the Great Pyramid; but the Great Pyramid was already

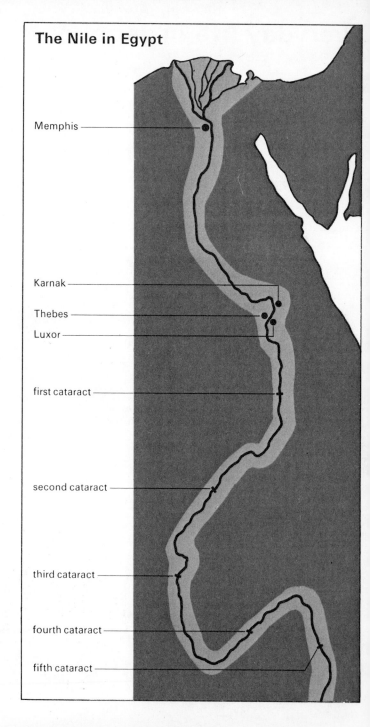

The Nile in Egypt

Memphis

Karnak

Thebes

Luxor

first cataract

second cataract

third cataract

fourth cataract

fifth cataract

A simple counter-balance took much of the strain out of raising water. The bucket was swung round and emptied into the upper irrigation ditch.

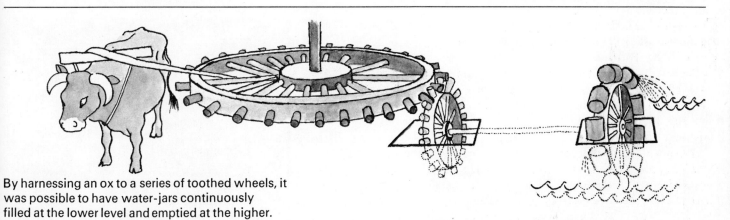

By harnessing an ox to a series of toothed wheels, it was possible to have water-jars continuously filled at the lower level and emptied at the higher.

The Archimedes screw was a device by which a stream of water could steadily be 'wound up'.

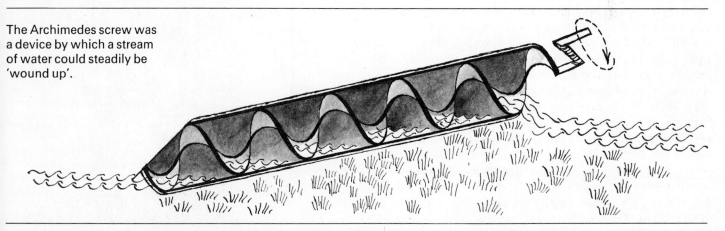

This painting is from the tomb of Amenmhat, at Thebes, and dates from about 1475 B.C. Amenmhat is in the centre; his song, written in heiroglyphs to his left, runs : 'A happy day, spending a happy morning'.

more than 2,000 years old when he was told that, and we cannot trust his figures. Anyway, it was a tremendous job.

Building Pyramids or keeping calendars would both be almost impossible without some means of noting things down, making records and sending messages. The Egyptians invented a form of picture-writing, and then improved it until each picture stood for a sound instead of for the thing it looked like. This sort of writing is called hieroglyphic. That is not a word which we use very often nowadays, but the next word connected with Egyptian writing is not so unusual. The Egyptians wrote on sheets which they made by glueing and pressing together strips of the inside of the papyrus reed. Though we make it in a different way now, you will recognize the word.

Talking about the Pyramids and writing has led us too far ahead. We must go back. Long before the Pyramids were built and before really good writing was invented, the people of Egypt had to learn to live together. Crowding into the Nile valley, the only fertile land for hundreds of miles around, they had to find some way of living side by side without always quarrelling and fighting. They seem to have found it best to have kings. We do not know exactly how it happened, but by about 3250 B.C. there were only two kingdoms in the Nile valley. Then Narmer, King of Upper Egypt, conquered Lower Egypt too. From that time onwards the whole land of Egypt was ruled by one king, or Pharaoh, and one of his titles was 'Lord of the Two Lands'.

The Egyptians had to pay for their king. The king did very important work. He made laws, so that all the Egyptians would

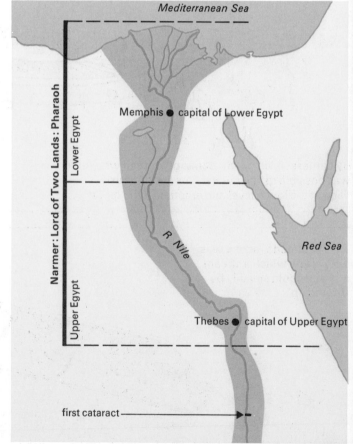

In this exact copy of an Egyptian painting, a nobleman is watching, on his estate, the work which supported both him and the Pharaoh. Paintings like this have often been found on the walls of the tombs of wealthy Egyptians, and give us much of our information about life in ancient Egypt.

live in peace, and, with the help of his noblemen, he saw that the laws were obeyed. He also led the Egyptian army, which protected the Nile valley from the wandering tribes of the desert lands, the sort of nomads we were talking about on page 23. In return for all this, the ordinary Egyptians had to keep the king, by giving to him and his nobles some of what they grew or made. Also they had to do as the king told them, and help him by working when he needed them. The pictures here are copies from Egyptian paintings and carvings, and show both labour and leisure.

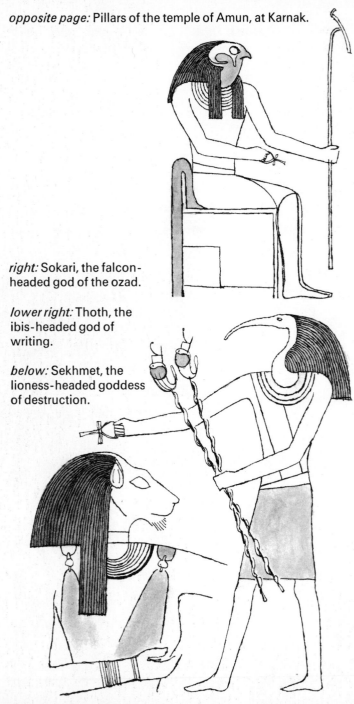

right: Sokari, the falcon-headed god of the ozad.

lower right: Thoth, the ibis-headed god of writing.

below: Sekhmet, the lioness-headed goddess of destruction.

It was not only Pharaoh and the nobles whom the Egyptians had to obey. There were also the gods.

You may remember that the Old Stone Age cave paintings probably had something to do with magic or even religion, but we could not be certain. We know more about the gods of the Egyptians. Each district had its own gods, and most of them seem to have been half-animal, like those shown here. Some of the gods were much more important than the others, and were worshipped all over Egypt. The most important of all the gods was Re, the sun-god. There were other very important gods who judged people after they were dead, and punished or rewarded them in the next world.

The Egyptians seem to have spent a great deal of time preparing for death and for what would happen to them afterwards. Everybody has heard of the mummies, and most people know that with the mummified body there would be buried all sorts of useful and precious things which the dead man or woman would need in the next world. Sometimes, if the real thing was too big to go into the tomb, a model would be put there instead. There were pictures, too.

From the tombs we have found out much of what we know about the Egyptians. Most of the Egyptian things which you can see in museums have been taken from tombs. In the tombs of the kings great treasures were placed. Only one of these royal tombs has been found with all its treasures still in it, the tomb of Tutankhamun. The picture on page 37 will give you an idea of the splendour with which a Pharaoh was surrounded in death as in life.

Together, the king and the gods were the masters of Egypt. The king was served by his nobles, his officials and his scribes. The gods were served by their priests and their scribes. These two sets of people worked well together. There was no quarrel between the king and the gods, because the king was himself a god. Once there was a king who said that there was only one true god, and tried to stop the worship of all the old ones. He failed. As soon as he was dead, the Egyptians went back to worshipping the gods they had always worshipped.

The ordinary Egyptians did as they were told. They did not ask questions. They believed in Pharaoh and the gods, and worked hard for them. We have already seen the skill and work that went into the Great Pyramid. Now look at the picture opposite of one of the temples which the men of Egypt built in honour of their gods and kings. All the stones had to be

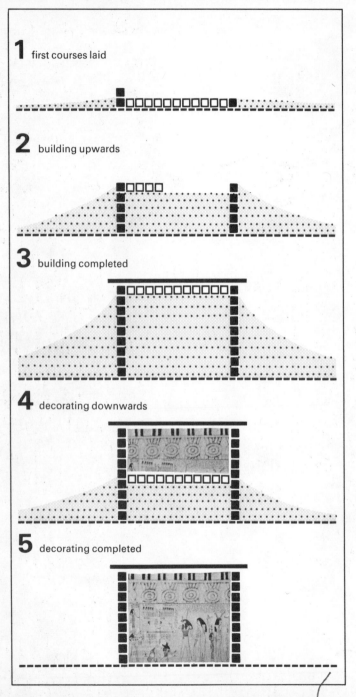

1 first courses laid

2 building upwards

3 building completed

4 decorating downwards

5 decorating completed

carved and carried without the help of modern machines, or even of steel tools. When it came to raising the high pillars of the temples, stone by stone, and putting on the roof, there was another problem. The Egyptians were very short of good timber, and could hardly build scaffolding that would be big and strong enough. It was easier and safer for them to raise the floor of a temple as they built it, shovelling in sand. When they had put on the roof they would start to shovel out the sand. As the floor sank, they would clean and paint the pillars and walls, until finally they reached the ground. These diagrams will make it clear to you.

In the British Museum there lies the left arm of a granite statue of an Egyptian king, broken off at the shoulder. The clenched fist measures eighteen inches across. The arm, from shoulder to knuckles, measures ten feet. You can compare this with your own arm.

We must take care not to start thinking that everything was always enormous in Egypt, with thousands of workmen needed for every job. Their huge buildings and statues show that the Egyptians could design and organize very well; it is not easy to keep thousands of men busy and to feed and house them. The Egyptians could do this, but they were just as good at little things. They were fine artists and careful craftsmen in gold, wood, bronze, paint, pottery, cloth and jewellery. They were not too busy to make toys for their children. The British Museum has, besides great stone figures, little clay and wooden dolls, and even a toy mouse with moving jaw and tail. They were skilled enough as surgeons to be able to mend a man's broken skull with an ivory patch.

The civilization of Ancient Egypt went on for nearly 3,000 years, and hundreds of books have been written about it. Here we have only a few pages to show what the Egyptians could do, and we shall have to be content with one more example – Egyptian ships.

One of the four goddesses, in gilded wood, guarding a chest containing part of the Pharaoh's remains, from the tomb of Tutankhamun.

The Egyptians seem never to have been very fond of the sea, though they lived by a great river. Still, they invented the world's first real ships.

As we saw when we were thinking about their buildings, the Egyptians were short of good timber. At first they were able to make boats out of bundles of reeds – the papyrus reed, which you have read of already. They tied these bundles very tightly at each end, and let them spread in the middle to form a kind of boat-shaped raft, like the one in the first picture below. Little boats like this were easy to make and very handy, and

Making a boat of papyrus reeds.

Making a boat of wood.

the Egyptians went on using them for a long time when only small boats were needed. They were not strong enough, though, to carry heavy loads, nor to support masts and sails, nor to sail on the open sea.

Now look at the picture opposite. It shows one of the ships which Queen Hatshepsut sent down the Red Sea to a land called Punt (possibly the land we call Somalia). You can count for yourself the differences between this ship and the reed boat, and you will find that you have a long list. There is one important thing that the picture does not explain. Because of the shortage of good timber, there was no skeleton of keel and ribs to hold the ship together. The Egyptians made the outside, the 'skin' of the ship with short, thick planks, held together by wooden pegs, as you can see in the small diagram opposite. But this did not make up for the lack of a good strong frame; the sides of the ship would probably sag outwards, and the ends would almost certainly sag downwards. The Egyptians tried to prevent this by putting beams across the ship, from side to side, just under the deck; can you see the ends of those beams sticking through the side of Queen Hatshepsut's ship? You can find easily the big rope that was used to prevent the ends of the ship from sagging. When they had a problem, the Egyptians usually found an answer.

Those ships went down the Red Sea. The Egyptians saw how useful it would be if the ships could sail all the way to the Nile. This would save the trouble of unloading, carrying the cargo across the desert, and loading once again into river boats. So they dug a canal. It was not, like the modern Suez Canal, from the Red Sea to the Mediterranean Sea, but where it would be more useful to the Egyptians. It ran from the Red Sea to the Nile.

As time went on, the Egyptians were able to reach lands where big trees grew, and to make stronger ships. At last they had to learn how to make warships. This, like the making of war-chariots, may have been something they learned from their enemies. But that brings us to another story altogether, and we shall have to put it off for a while.

The Egyptians began simply as New Stone Age farmers on the banks of the Nile, and we have seen only a few of the things they made and did. While they were building up their great civilization, most of the people in the world were still living New or even Old Stone Age lives.

far right: How a ship's planks were pegged together.

A ship of Queen Hatshepsut, redrawn from a tomb picture.

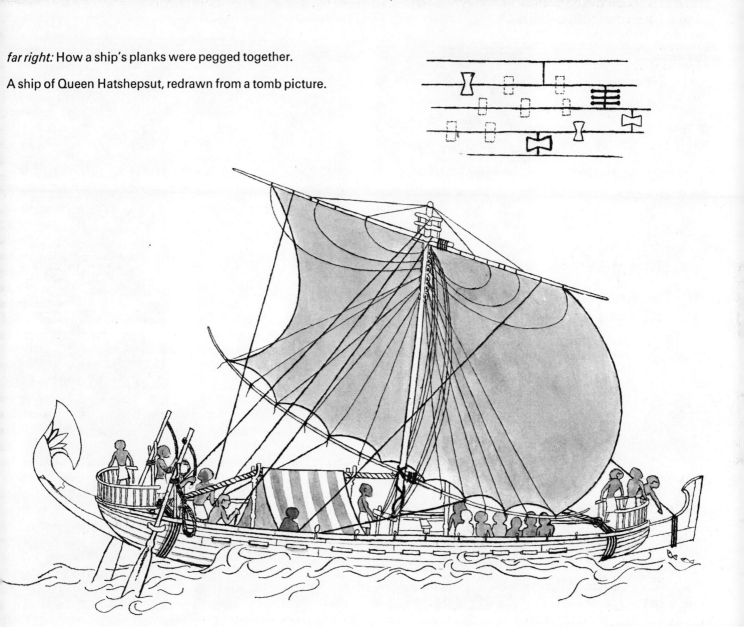

Here are some objects which show the art of four different areas of civilization over a period of 2,000 years.

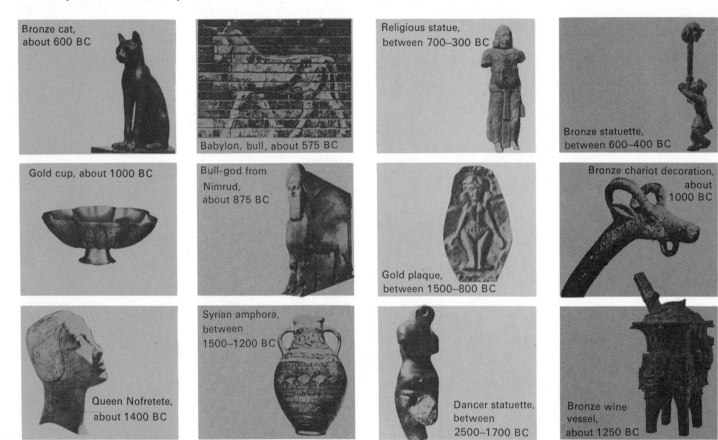

Bronze cat, about 600 BC

Babylon, bull, about 575 BC

Religious statue, between 700–300 BC

Bronze statuette, between 600–400 BC

Gold cup, about 1000 BC

Bull-god from Nimrud, about 875 BC

Gold plaque, between 1500–800 BC

Bronze chariot decoration, about 1000 BC

Queen Nofretete, about 1400 BC

Syrian amphora, between 1500–1200 BC

Dancer statuette, between 2500–1700 BC

Bronze wine vessel, about 1250 BC

Imhotep, designed the first pyramid, about 2500 BC

Bronze from Nineveh, between 2400–2290

Dancing girl, between 2400–2000 BC

Earthenware, between 2500–2000 BC

Great civilizations began, and flourished, while in the rest of the world prehistory continued.

Between the rivers

Eastwards from Egypt there is desert for 700 miles. Then, in the middle of barren wilderness, there are the twin valleys of two great rivers, the Tigris and the Euphrates. Look back at the map of the Middle East on page 24, and you will see all this. You will also see that, as they wind through the plain, the two rivers gradually come together. (Now they join before they reach the sea, but that had not happened 5,000 years ago.) Near the sea the rivers had made big muddy marshes. Here people came to live, and they built huts from the reeds which grew in the marshes.

The land between the two rivers is usually called Mesopotamia; the name comes from two Greek words, 'meso' meaning 'middle', and 'potamos' meaning 'river'. The southern part used to be called Babylonia, and the part nearest of all to the river mouths was called Sumer.

There grew up in Sumer and Babylonia a great civilization which depended, as in Egypt, on the waters of the rivers. The mud from the rivers provided more than good soil for the crops. It provided the only plentiful building material, because both stone and wood were very scarce. In Egypt many of the houses had been built of mud bricks, but, as you know, the greatest buildings were of stone. In the land of the two rivers the builders had to use mud bricks for everything. This, as you can see from the picture, does not mean that they had to be content with little things. Some of the early parts of the Bible are about the people who lived in this land, and it is easy to see how some great temple-tower in Babylonia may have been the beginning of the story of the Tower of Babel.

Sometimes the people of Sumer got more mud than they wanted. The floods were not so regular as they were in Egypt, and sometimes they were very high. Again we are reminded of the Bible. While digging up buried cities of Sumer, archaeologists have sometimes found, between the ruins of one city and the ruins of the city that came before it, a thick layer of river-mud. Only the most terrible flood could have risen high enough above the plain to do this. In those days the Sumerians knew nothing of the world beyond their plain, and the mountains and deserts which surrounded it. To them, the

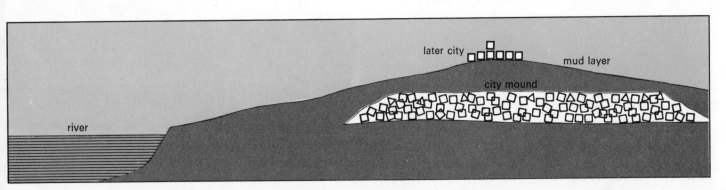

later city   mud layer

city mound

river

41

land of the two rivers really was the world, and a flood which swept away all the cities would indeed destroy the world. So the story of Noah is not at all a silly one. The story in the Bible is not the only one about it. A hundred years ago some books were found in the ruins of one of these cities, telling the story of how the gods decided to wipe out mankind with a flood, and how only one man, with his family and animals, was saved. According to this story the man's name was Uta-napishtim, not Noah.

The books, too, were made of mud. They were tablets of mud, with the words written on while the mud was wet, then baked like bricks. The marks on the mud were made, not by scratching, but by jabbing with the end of a reed that had been carefully cut to a small sharp triangle. This made wedge-shaped marks in the mud, and this sort of writing is called cuneiform; the Latin word for 'wedge' is 'cuneus'. Cuneiform was still picture-writing of a sort, but you can see from the chart below how the signs changed from pictures which anybody could recognize to cuneiform words which a scribe could jab quickly into the mud, and which only a scribe could read.

This picture shows you what the people of Babylon, Ur and the other famous cities used to seal their letters. Remembering that the letters were written on mud, you will easily see how the seals were used. They worked in the same way as the rotary presses which print modern newspapers.

Cuneiform writing was made up of straight lines, and this made it easy to cut into stone or metal. We have been dealing with mud because it was so important to these people, and

A scribe writing cuneiform, using a sharp reed pen on a damp clay tablet.

How cuneiform developed.

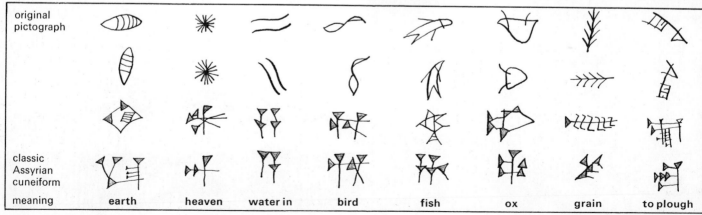

| meaning | earth | heaven | water in | bird | fish | ox | grain | to plough |

42

because it shows you how they were clever enough to use it for food, houses and writing. We must not forget that they learned to use all sorts of other materials when they were able to get them. You can see this from the elaborate jewellery of a court lady shown in the picture.

Have you noticed that we have mentioned cities often, but never a king who ruled over the whole land? The king whose queen and her attendants wore such jewellery was king only of one city, Ur. The people of the land of the two rivers did not learn to live together as well as the people of the Nile. The cities often fought against one another, until one would become strong enough to make the others obey.

If you look at the next map you will see how the land was full of cities. They rose and they fell. Sometimes one would be the most important, sometimes another. Gradually the leadership moved northwards, away from cities like Ur and Lagash, towards Babylon, and then beyond.

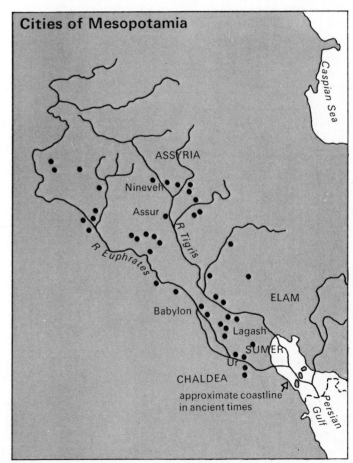

Law-making and war-making

We shall not try to follow all the ups and downs of the various cities, but there are two very important things which we ought to know about. One, law, was good; the other, war, was not.

Every city was supposed to belong to a god. The king and the priests were the servants of the god, and they told the ordinary people what the god wanted them to do. The ordinary people did as they were told.

When the king of one city conquered others, he would have to make sure that all the people in all the cities knew what to do. He would have to see that they all had rules to follow, so that they would live peacefully together. The first important set of rules – or code of laws, to give the correct name – which has been discovered was made by a king called Hammurabi, who was king of Babylon nearly 2,000 years B.C. Here is a picture of the code of laws. It is a large stone, covered with cuneiform writing. Perhaps it does not look very interesting, but it is important. Try to think of what it would be like if we had no laws. You would have no rights if the law had not given them to you. If it were not for the laws, anybody could do any bad thing that he wished. You can imagine what it would be like.

There were 282 laws in Hammurabi's code, and they covered everything that seemed likely to be important. There were laws on witchcraft, robbery, buying and selling, hiring, debt, inheritance, divorce, adoption, rates of wages, compensation for loss or injury. In all these Hammurabi did his best to make sure of two things; the man who had done wrong should pay for it, and the man who had suffered should be paid. Here are a few examples of the sort of thing that Hammurabi ordered:

'IF A MAN has given his boat to a boatman on hire, if the boatman has been careless, has grounded the boat or destroyed it, the boatman shall give a boat to the owner of the boat in compensation.'

'IF A BUILDER has built a house for some-one and has not made his work firm, and if the house he built has fallen and has killed the owner of the house, that builder shall be put to death. . . . If it has destroyed property, he shall restore everything he destroyed; and because the house he built was not

The stele, or inscribed upright stone, with the laws of Hammurabi. At the top the king is shown receiving the symbols of authority, a rod and ring, from the sun god.

firm and fell in, out of his own funds he shall rebuild the house that fell.'

'IF ONE destroys the eye of a free-born man, his eye shall one destroy.'

'IF THE ROBBER is not caught, the man who has been robbed shall make claim . . . and the town and its governor . . . shall give back to him everything that he has lost.'

Nowadays many people would say that some of the laws of Hammurabi were too hard, too rough-and-ready. But they were fair, they were intended to protect honest men, and everybody could find out exactly what the law was. An ordinary Babylonian had no say in making or changing the laws, but he knew what the laws were and he knew that the laws were as fair as the king could make them. Later, people were to start thinking that the king himself was bound by the laws.

For many years Babylon remained the greatest city in all Mesopotamia. Then, in the north, there arose a stern and fierce people called the Assyrians, who seem to have delighted only in war and bloodshed. There had been wars ever since civilization began; perhaps men have always fought, ever since the beginning of the Old Stone Age. There was something about the Assyrians, however, which seems especially horrible. Judge for yourself.

Assyrian kings built for themselves, in various Assyrian cities, great palaces. The palaces were built of mud bricks, of course, but the walls were faced with flat slabs of stone on which pictures were carved. Many of these carved stones have been dug up from the ruins of the buried cities, and a large number have been set up again on the walls of rooms in the British Museum. We can go there and see the sort of pictures that the Assyrian kings liked to look at, and it seems that they enjoyed two things most of all, hunting and warfare: killing animals and killing men.

Here is a picture of the king hunting lions. See how he displays iron nerve and unerring skill in whichever method of killing he chooses. On horse or on foot, with sword, spear or

Assyrian
carvings,
from Nineveh.

45

bow, he is a master killer. To understand the Assyrians better, compare the next two pictures. One is from the same lion-hunting carvings, and shows a dying lioness snarling at the hunters. The Assyrian artist has stressed both the savage courage of the beast and the deadly wounds. The other picture is not of an Assyrian carving, but of an Egyptian statue. Here the artist has also been able to show the great strength of the lion, but instead of blood and savagery he has stressed the lion's kingly dignity.

Assyrians move a colossal statue. The gangs of labourers
are dressed differently, probably to show that each gang
is composed of captives from a different conquered nation.

In warfare the kings of Assyria took just as much pleasure, and perhaps more. Carving after carving shows us the king defeating his enemies and taking their cities. We see the chariots, the bowmen, the engineers with their battering-rams and mining devices, all in great detail. Apart from some scenes showing religious ceremonial, or the building of a palace, all these wall-carvings seem to be of hunting or of war. Even in the building scenes, the most obvious thing is usually the crowd of labourers who are dragging the huge blocks of stone, doubtless slaves taken in war. It is true that other peoples besides the Assyrians have decorated their walls with pictures of war and hunting, but the Assyrians hardly seem to have been able to think of anything else.

The Assyrians also seem to have tried to spread terror. This may have been partly to frighten and weaken their enemies, but it looks very much as though they were also naturally cruel. Some of the battle carvings show the Assyrian soldiers beheading their enemies and counting the heads. In some of their cuneiform inscriptions the Assyrian kings boast about the number of captives whom they have had crucified, impaled or skinned alive.

Vast empires

We have seen two of the areas where civilization began, Egypt and Mesopotamia. We have seen how the peoples who lived there learned many things, from writing and building cities to fighting and conquering. Though, as you can see if you look back to the maps on page 24, other peoples were making themselves civilized in India and China, these other civilizations were far away; in most parts of the world people were still Prehistoric, living Old Stone Age or New Stone Age lives. But Egypt and Mesopotamia were fairly close together. You can see this from the second map on page 24. If you look at that, and at the first map on this page, you will see that it was not necessary to cross the desert to go from one of these civilizations to the other. There was a curved strip of less barren land, which has been called 'the Fertile Crescent'.

On this Fertile Crescent there was pasture for flocks and herds. There was land for farms and cities. It was easy to travel, and this was true both for peaceful merchants and for ramies.

You already know about one of the early cities which was built there – Jericho. You probably know from the Bible about another people who settled there – the Jews. Though Abraham lived once in Ur, his people were nomads, and after many adventures in the desert, in Egypt, and outside the walls of Jericho itself, they settled down where you see them on the map, about Jerusalem.

We can learn much from the Bible about the peoples of the ancient Middle East. You may remember how King Solomon made friends with King Hiram of Tyre, and was helped by him in building the great Temple. Tyre was a city of the people called Phoenicians, and they were very famous merchants: that is why they were able to help Solomon to get precious things for his Temple. The Phoenicians were the first people, as far as we know, to make their living almost entirely by trading by sea. Their ships explored and traded all round the Mediterranean Sea, and even beyond. The cities of the Phoenicians became rich and strong, and the Phoenicians were satisfied with this. They were sailors, not soldiers, and do not seem to have had any interest in trying to conquer more land.

Anyway, the time came when the smaller peoples of the Middle East had little chance in war. Powerful armies from

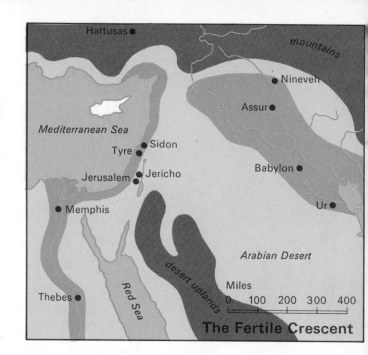

The Fertile Crescent

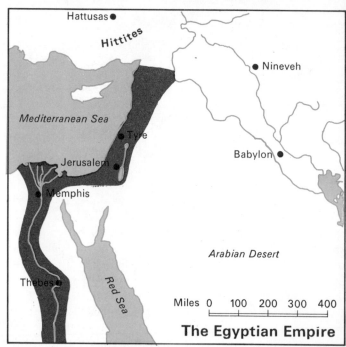

The Egyptian Empire

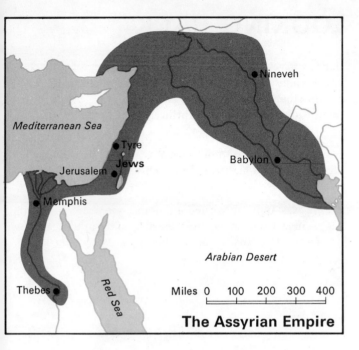

The Assyrian Empire

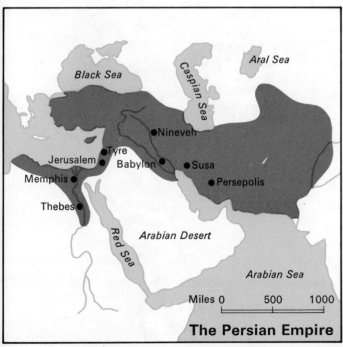

The Persian Empire

mighty empires began to roll over the Fertile Crescent, and when the dust of their battles died away it was wisest for the smaller peoples to obey the conquerors. Vast empires were now being made.

These maps will show you what happened. The Egyptians were the first to send their conquering armies into Palestine and Syria. They did it because they had been themselves conquered by nomads who had come into Egypt from that direction. The Egyptians learned from these tribesmen the use of war-chariots, rose up against them, and at last drove them out. Then the Egyptians decided that to protect their own land in future they would have to hold Palestine.

This was only the beginning. The Egyptians found that they now had to face new enemies, like the Hittites who had a strong kingdom farther north. Years went by, the Hittites were wiped out by other enemies and the Egyptians became less strong, but new conquerors came. You will not be surprised to see what the Assyrians were able to do. It was during their conquests that the ten lost tribes of Israel were taken away; this cruel idea of uprooting people from their homes and forcing them to go to strange lands has been used by many conquerors since then.

Finally there arose new conquerors from the high lands to the east of Mesopotamia – the Persians. Look very carefully at the map of their empire. You will see that it is the biggest of all. The Persians were mighty warriors. It may be, too, that many of the peoples in this part of the world let themselves be conquered without much of a fight; they were getting used to being part of some big empire or other, and they did not care very much who the new rulers were. Whatever the main reason was, the Persian kings ruled over all the civilized lands of the Middle East, over Egypt, Mesopotamia, over all the old famous cities. Between the seas, the deserts and the high mountain ranges the Persian armies had conquered all. To a thoughtful Persian it must have seemed that outside the Persian Empire there existed only barren lands and poor uncivilized men, and that all those peoples who had created civilization were now gathered together in one vast empire.

49

1

LOOKING BACK

In a few pages we have gone through the story of how people first became civilized. It is such an important story and the changes that it describes were so great that we ought to make sure of it before we go any further.

1 For hundreds of thousands of years men lived a very hard life, hunting and gathering food. This was the Old Stone Age.

2 It was only about ten thousand years ago that some people invented farming, and were able to begin to settle down in villages. This was the New Stone Age.

2

3

4

3, 4   After this, some people living in the valleys of great rivers began to make new things very quickly, and to live a civilized life. We saw some of the things that the peoples of Egypt and Mesopotamia did. Because they discovered how to read and write, and we can read their writing, we know enough about them to include them in History instead of Prehistory.

These civilized peoples obeyed their gods, their kings and their laws.

5

5   Cities and kingdoms fought against one another and conquered one another until at last there was only one big empire covering all the civilized lands of the Middle East.

6

6   With the setting up of that great empire, it looks as though we have come to the end of a story. But in History the end of one story is usually the beginning of another. It is time now to leave the ancient civilizations of the Middle East and to look at some people who lived just outside the great Persian Empire.

3. THE GREEKS

The early Greeks: legends and questions

Nearly everybody has heard about the siege of Troy and the wooden horse, and of the wanderings of Ulysses when Troy had been taken. These are two of the most famous tales of the ancient Greeks. There was a long poem, or epic, about each of them. The 'Iliad' told the story of Troy, or Ilium as it was called in Greek, and the 'Odyssey' told the story of Ulysses, or Odysseus, to give him his correct Greek name. These poems are supposed to have been composed by a blind poet called Homer, and they are still very popular today. The Greeks themselves thought of Homer's epics rather as we think of the finest works of our chief poet, Shakespeare.

You have probably heard many of the other famous stories of the ancient Greeks – of Perseus and the Gorgons, of the labours of Hercules, of the voyage of Jason and the Argonauts in quest of the Golden Fleece, of Theseus and the Minotaur. They are fine stories, and they are very old. They are legends though, and not factual accounts of what really did take place. Does this mean that there is no truth in any of them? Even from legends we can pick up many ideas about how and why people behave, but can we take any of these stories further? Was there such a place as Troy, for instance, and did the Greeks capture it?

How Troy was found is one of the most exciting stories of archaeological discovery that you could read, and it is a pity that there is no room to tell it in full here. Very briefly, a strange German merchant called Heinrich Schliemann, about a hundred years ago, dug into a great mound in the place where, according to the old tales, Troy was supposed to be. He found buried cities and treasure. Then he went to the old city of Mycenae, where the leaders of the Greeks were said to have lived. Once again, he did it. This time the gold was in the graves of long-dead warriors, golden masks like the one opposite covering the face of each hero.

Of course, this does not prove that all the epic of the Trojan

War is true. But Troy was there, and there were warrior-chiefs among these early Greeks. The Myceneans, though, as these Greeks are known nowadays, were different from the 'classical' Greeks we shall be discussing in the rest of this book, the Greeks whose civilization has done so much to make our own. If you compare this warrior of about 1400 B.C. with the soldier on page 64, you will see some big differences.

There is another amazing story of archaeological discovery about the early Greeks. This time it took place on the island of Crete, and the discoverer was an Englishman called Arthur Evans. Beginning where Schliemann left off, he found at a place called Knossos the remains of a civilization which had been completely lost and forgotten. Who were these people? Were they early Greeks? Look at these pictures, and see how different they look from the Greeks in the rest of this book. The Minoans, as they have been named, after the legend of King Minos of Crete, had their own ways of writing, which at first baffled everyone who studied it. Yet when at last a scholar tried fitting Greek words to these mysterious alphabets – it worked; but only with one of them. Were the Minoans Greek after all? If not, what made them use Greek? Did the Greeks get some of their civilization from the Minoans? Nobody knows the answers.

The picture below shows you one of the strangest customs of the people of ancient Crete. To judge from pictures like this, the bull was a sacred animal, and young men and women had to perform difficult and dangerous acrobatics with it. How does this fit in with the Theseus story? Was he one of the acrobats?

Did the priest in Knossos wear a bull-head mask, as the pre-historic man on page 17 wears a stag's head? Is that what lies behind the legend of the Minotaur?

This part of Greek history is full of unanswered questions, and we can only guess how much the Greeks who came afterwards owed to the Myceneans and Minoans.

A Cretan lady and gentleman, redrawn from paintings at Knossos.

Bull acrobats, redrawn from paintings at Knossos.

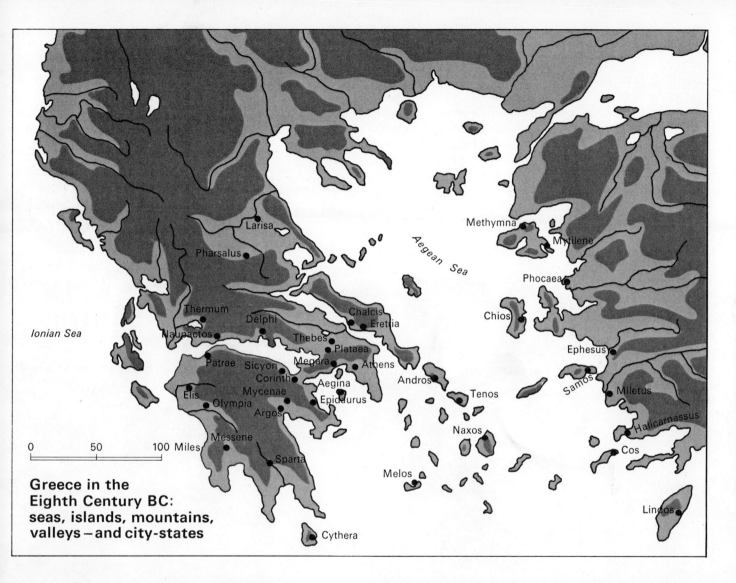

Greece in the Eighth Century BC: seas, islands, mountains, valleys – and city-states

Map labels: Larisa, Pharsalus, Methymna, Mytilene, Aegean Sea, Phocaea, Thermum, Delphi, Chalcis, Eretria, Chios, Naupactos, Ionian Sea, Thebes, Plataea, Patrae, Sicyon, Megara, Athens, Ephesus, Corinth, Aegina, Andros, Samos, Elis, Mycenae, Epidaurus, Tenos, Miletus, Olympia, Argos, Halicarnassus, Messene, Naxos, Cos, Sparta, Melos, Lindos, Cythera

Scale: 0 50 100 Miles

The little states of the Greeks

When we were thinking about the Egyptians and Mesopotamians we saw how important geography was to them. It was just as important to the Greeks. But instead of living beside a great river the Greeks lived as you see on this map. Their land is cut up by the sea and the mountains, so that the people have to live on islands or in valleys or on little plains quite separate from one another.

In their valley or on their island the Greeks who lived there often built a city. Though they might make a living by farming or fishing, in the fields or on the sea, the city was their centre. In the city they could all meet and talk – Greeks were great talkers – and decide how they thought their city should be run.

The Greeks liked to live in little states of this sort, city-states as we call them. (The Greek name for such a state was 'polis', and you may be able to work out which modern English words come from that Greek word.) They liked a state to be small enough for all the citizens to know what was going on, and to know the ruler or rulers personally. Some Greeks went further. They believed that all the citizens should be able to meet together to decide how their rulers were behaving and to change them if they were not doing well enough. It is obvious that nothing like this could be done in a big state like Egypt or Persia, so these Greeks did not want to live in a big state. This impression may give you a rough idea of what a Greek city-state, or polis, was like.

Every Greek wanted to be free, and thought that no man could be free if he had to do just as he was told by someone who lived far away and simply gave orders. A Greek liked to be able to ask questions. He wanted to know WHY. If he did not agree with what his rulers said, he wanted to be able to go and see them and argue with them. It is easy to understand how a Greek would not want some far-away king to rule over his city-state.

New city-states

If a Greek did not want other people to rule over his city, he knew that other Greeks would feel the same about their cities. This idea that each city-state would be free and would look after itself is one of the things we notice about their colonies.

The map shows you how the Greeks spread their colonies round the Mediterranean Sea between about 800 and 500 B.C. You can see how there was a specially large number of these colonies in Sicily and in Southern Italy. It would have been hard, anyway, for a city beside the Aegean Sea to keep a tight hold on a new city so far away, but the 'mother' cities do not seem to have tried to keep control over their 'children'. The citizens of the new city might feel a special friendship for the old city, but the new city would be a free city.

Some of these new cities became very much richer and stronger than some of the old ones.

Greek colonization : Mother-cities and Daughter-cities.
Only the main Mother-cities are named.

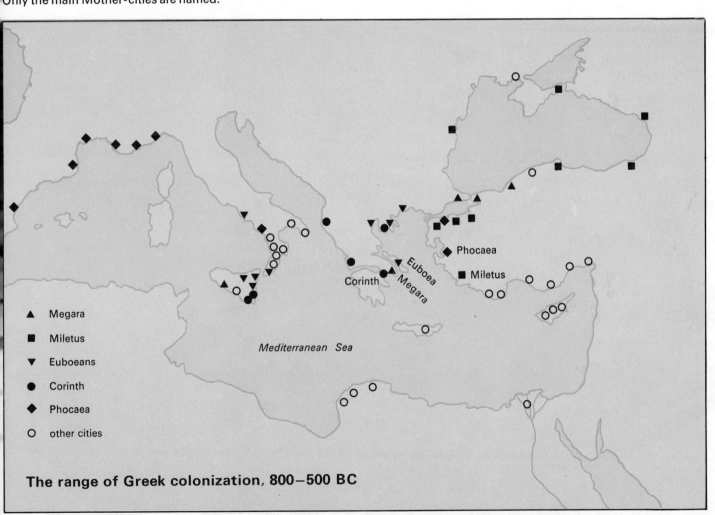

Megara
Miletus
Euboeans
Corinth
Phocaea
other cities

The range of Greek colonization, 800–500 BC

Why did the Greeks found so many new cities? It is difficult to be sure. Sometimes the people who founded the colony may not have liked the people who were ruling the old city. Sometimes the old city had been conquered by an enemy, and the citizens would not stay to be ruled by a foreigner. Most often, though, it may have been over-population which sent some of these Greeks to found new city-states. What it means is this:

Suppose that more and more children are born, so that more and more people live in the state. This increase in population, as it is called, could go on until the land could not provide a good living for everybody. Greeks usually did not expect luxury. They were quite happy with food, clothes and houses which would seem rough and simple for most of us today. But still, they had to live. This problem of over-population is one that you will find very often in history. It may be solved by finding new ways of earning a living – trading, or making things, for instance. It may also be solved by finding more land; if the land is empty, this is easy, but if there are other people there already, it means fighting, killing and robbing. Perhaps the Greeks who went to found colonies had to be ready to do all of these things. Greeks could be very hard.

A merchant ship and a war galley.
From an Athenian cup of about 520 B.C.
Some authorities think the
galley is a pirate ship.

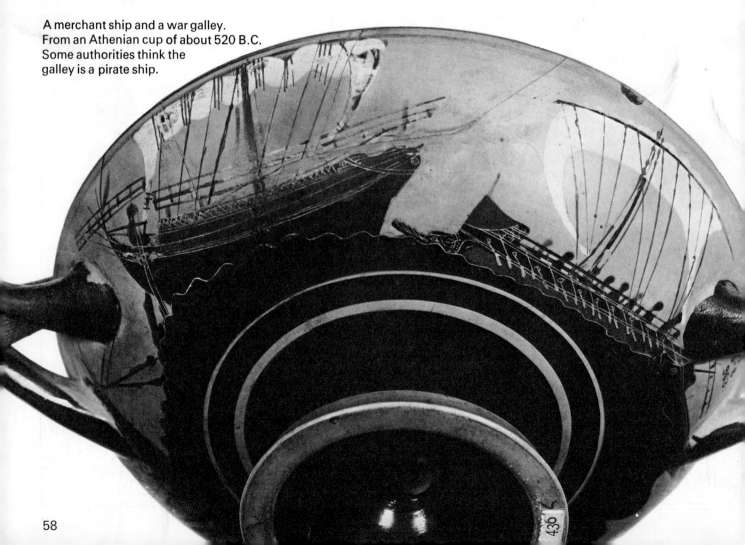

58

On their trading voyages around the shores of the Mediterranean, Greeks sold oil, wine, pottery of all sorts and bronze goods.

1
This amphora is typical of the wine jars carried by Greek traders, who ranged from the Crimea in the East, to Spain in the West.

2
This bronze horse and rider, discovered at Grumentum, in Southern Italy was made about 500 B.C.

3
An East Greek vase, decorated with wine jars, dating from about 550 B.C. It was found at Ponticapaeum, in the Crimea.

4
A Chalcidean vase of the black figure style of East Greece, a type which sold well in Etruria and Southern Italy. It dates from the later sixth century B.C.

 Sometimes the state was ruled by a king, by a *monarch*. (*Monos* is Greek for 'one'; *Arkho* is Greek for 'rule'.)

 Sometimes the state was ruled by a few men, by *oligarchs*. (*Oligoi* is Greek for 'few'.)

 Sometimes the state was ruled by the 'best' people, by *aristocrats*. (*Aristos* is Greek for 'best'; *Kratos* is Greek for 'power'.)

 Sometimes the state was ruled by all the citizens, by *democrats*. (*Demos* is Greek for 'the people'.)

 Sometimes things got into such a mess that it looked as if there was *anarchy*, or no rule at all.

 Sometimes, when things were going badly, one man would be allowed to take over the power in a state, even though he had no right to do so; he was called a *tyrant*.

(All these words are still used, though the meanings are sometimes slightly different from what the Greeks would have understood.

Free citizens

The Greeks liked to be free, and that was why they preferred to live in small city-states. These states could be ruled in different ways, and any one state could be ruled in different ways at different times.

From all this you will see that the Greeks were not like the older civilized peoples, the Egyptians and Mesopotamians, who were content to do as they were told by their kings and priests. Greeks were usually ready to try out something new, and very ready to ask questions.

The Greeks asked questions about all sorts of things. They looked at the world around them, and they wondered how and why it worked. They looked at the people in the world, and tried to work out how men should behave towards one another. Trying to find out the answers, they began what we call Science and Philosophy. Instead of simply believing all the stories about their gods and goddesses, some of the Greeks

tried to make sense of them. To a Greek, anything that did not make sense should not be believed, and the Greek would try to discover what the truth really was. You may be interested in the ideas that some of the Greeks had, when they stopped being satisfied by the stories about their gods. For example, one of their philosophers had the idea that everything was made of tiny atoms; he did not have the instruments to prove it, but modern scientists agree that he was quite right.

The thing to remember is that, as far as we know, the Greeks were the first people to have the idea that a free man was entitled to ask as many questions as he liked. Of course, not all the Greeks spent their time arguing about science and philosophy. Some were lazy, some were stupid, some were sure that they knew the truth already; there are good and bad in all nations. They were not perfect, but they had this to teach the world:

A FREE MAN THINKS FOR HIMSELF

Some were not free

Like most of the old civilized peoples, the Greeks kept slaves. There were many slaves in a Greek polis. Usually the Greeks seem to have treated their slaves quite well, but we ought to remember that so many Greeks had time to spend discussing and helping to rule their city-states only because slaves were doing much of their work for them.

Today we do not need slaves. We have machines to do a lot of the hard and dull and dirty work for us. If the Greeks had owned such machines, would they have set their slaves free? Perhaps, but perhaps not. The Greeks did not believe that all men were equal. One of their greatest philosophers and scientists, Aristotle, thought it obvious that some people would never be fit to be anything but slaves; mankind was divided into two great classes, those who had the minds of citizens, and those who had the minds of slaves.

Apart from slaves, there were others who were not supposed to be fit to help in running the city-state. Women, children and foreigners (no matter how long they had lived in the state) could not be citizens. Only a fraction of the people living in a Greek polis were citizens. The numbers of free women and children, foreigners and slaves who lived in a Greek city-state probably varied from time to time and from city to city, and we have no exact figures at all; but the diagram gives you a rough idea of how the population may have been made up.

If you ever try to imagine what it would have been like to live, not in the twentieth century A.D., but in some other period of History, you should always try to imagine where you would have been in a diagram like that.

All the same, the important thing is not that there were many people who were not citizens. The important thing about the Greeks is that they had the idea that the citizens could share in running the state, and not just obey the orders of one man. Once the idea had been invented, there was always the chance that it might spread, and that more people might get the opportunity to become citizens.

The population of a polis has to be guessed from odd pieces of evidence, because we have no reliable figures. This diagram represents Athens in the time of Pericles. Athens was exceptionally big, rich and democratic. Her population may have been about 300,000, when other polis were only one-fifth of this size, and many were much smaller still.

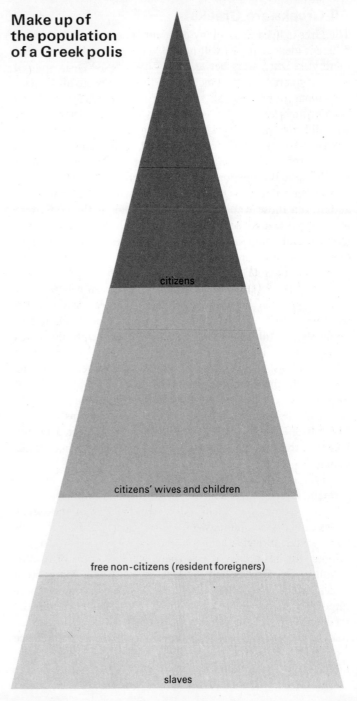

Make up of the population of a Greek polis

citizens

citizens' wives and children

free non-citizens (resident foreigners)

slaves

All Greeks are Greeks

The Greeks lived in so many different states and had so many different ideas that you will not be very surprised to hear that there were often wars between the city-states. Yet, in spite of all their quarrels, they remembered that they were all Greeks.

For one thing, they all spoke the same language, and had been brought up on the mighty poems of Homer. Other people who did not speak Greek, whose languages just sounded like 'Bar-Bar-Bar-Bar-Bar', were all called 'barbarians'. Some of these barbarians, the Greeks knew, were great and civilized peoples, like the Egyptians. But they were not Greeks.

Another thing was that the Greeks worshipped the same gods; even those who had their doubts about the gods were usually polite and sensible enough to show respect to the temples and religious services. All Greeks, and some non-Greeks, too, honoured the famous oracle at Delphi, where the priestess of the god Apollo was supposed to be given the power to foretell the future. Many clever and wise men believed that this was possible, because they thought that Fate had decided what was going to happen, and that no man could change it. Some people still believe this. But sometimes the prophecy was not very clear. There was the famous example of the powerful King Croesus of Lydia, who wondered whether or not he should fight the Persians. The oracle told him that if he went to war he would destroy a great empire. Full of confidence, he attacked the Persians, but the empire destroyed was his own. Perhaps one of the reasons why the Greeks respected Delphi was that the god told the truth only to those who had brains enough to see it.

As the map shows, there was another place where the gods brought Greeks together. At Olympia, every four years, the Olympic Games were held. Athletes from any of the Greek states came to run, jump, wrestle, drive chariots. They did this because they thought that it pleased the gods, and also to gain honour for their city-states. There were no rich prizes for winning. The Greeks had the idea of sport as a competition which brings rivals together as friends, where it is much more important to do your best honestly than to contrive by all means to win. These games were thought to be so important that, if there was a war between some of the cities, a truce would be declared to allow the athletes and spectators to attend the Olympic Games.

The Greeks thought of themselves, despite all their differ-

right: A minstrel, who would recite the tales of Homer from memory, shown on an Athenian wine-jar of about 480 B.C.

far right. The Athenian treasury at Delphi, built near the end of the sixth century B.C.

ences and disagreements, as the same sort of people, and different from the other civilized peoples. You have already read enough to have some ideas about whether or not they were right to think this. Now, about 500 B.C., the great test was coming to them. The Persian Empire, as you saw on page 49, covered the older civilized lands; now it was ready to swallow up the Greek city-states. Would they all see the danger? Would they be able to stop their own quarrels and unite against Persia? Was Persia so strong that it would be hopeless to fight? Each city-state had to give its own answers.

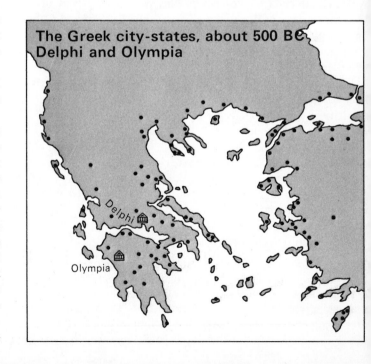

The Greek city-states, about 500 B.C.
Delphi and Olympia

Delphi

Olympia

62

Young athletes on a sculpture of about
510 B.C.

The Persian Wars

If you look at the map on page 49 and then at the map on page 62, you will see something about the part of Asia Minor which touches the Aegean Sea. There are Greek cities there, and it is part of the Persian Empire.

Inside the Persian Empire everyone did exactly what the Great King said. Even the highest nobles fell on their faces before the king, to show how low they were when compared with him. You can guess what the Greeks thought of this. The Greek cities in the Persian Empire rose in revolt, and sent across the Aegean Sea to ask for help from other Greek cities. Some, especially Athens and Eretria, did send help. But in spite of this, King Darius of Persia was much too strong. He crushed the rebels. Then he thought that he had better make sure that the Greeks on the islands and the mainland of Greece would not bother him again. He would add them to his empire.

Events before Marathon

Persian messengers came to each Greek city, demanding earth and water, as a sign that all the land and water of the city belonged to Darius. Some cities thought that the Persians were so strong that it was best to give in at once. The men of Athens and Sparta, though, were so angry that they even forgot that messengers should never be harmed. In Athens the Persian envoys were thrown into prison. In Sparta the Persians were thrown down a well, with the remark that they would find plenty of earth and water at the bottom.

The first fleet that Darius had sent to Greece had been wrecked in a storm. Now, in 490 B.C., he sent another fleet.

carrying a strong army which had special orders to capture Eretria and Athens. Eretria was the first to be attacked. Athens sent help, and meanwhile asked the Spartans for the help they had promised. But the messenger, Pheidippides, came back with bad news. The Spartans, though they were the best soldiers in Greece, had got the idea that the gods did not wish them to begin a war before the next full moon; so they were waiting until then.

The Athenians could not wait. Eretria had fallen. The Persians had landed at Marathon. You can see the position on this map. With the help of 1,000 men from the little city of Plataea, the Athenians gave battle.

There are no figures that we can really trust for the size of the armies. What seems certain is that the Persian army was so much bigger than the Athenian army that it would be able to surround it. But the Athenians had one advantage. Their men were much more heavily armed than most of the Persians.

You can see the details of Athenian armour in the picture on page 64. Now try to imagine a long line of these men, all standing shoulder to shoulder, holding their shields in front of them and with their heavy spears thrust forward. Behind this line of men are hundreds more, ready to give support and to take the places of those who fall dead or wounded. It would look like a solid wall of bronze and thick leather, bristling with spear-points. The picture below gives you an impression of what a phalanx – that is the name of a solid body of soldiers like this – would look like to the enemy. The Greeks were used to this sort of fighting. The Persians were not. The Persians had many different sorts of warriors in their army, on horse and on foot, armed in many different ways and used to many different sorts of fighting. Above all, the Persians had good archers.

Battle of Marathon

Very few of them, however, were heavily enough armed to fight in phalanx style.

Because of this, the Athenian general, a man called Miltiades, thought that in a straight battle, front to front, his men could probably drive the Persians back. What he feared was that the Persians might be able to get round the sides and back of his army. He had to try to prevent this, and this sketch-map shows you how he did it: hills, marsh, felled trees.

As soon as they were ready, so as not to give the Persians

time to shoot too many arrows at them, the men of Athens charged. As they went forward some of them thought they saw an owl flying ahead of them – the sacred bird of their goddess Athene. Whether or not they felt that the gods were with them, it could not have been a very quick charge. The Athenians relied on keeping together and using their steady weight. When the armies came together there was a terrible struggle. The Persians fought so well that they broke through the Athenian phalanx in one place. At last the heavy arms of the Athenians were too much for the Persians. They turned and fled to their ships, and the fleet put to sea.

According to the Athenians, 6,400 Persians lay dead on the battle-field, and 192 Athenians had fallen. Even if the figures are exaggerated, it was a great victory, and Athens never forgot it. You can see on this coin how the helmet of Athene was decorated with the laurels of victory; how her owl spread its wings as it had done over the battle-field of Marathon.

The most famous tale of Marathon, as you have probably heard, is the story of how the news was carried to Athens. The runner (some say he was that same Pheidippides who had run

A Greek killing a Persian, from an Athenian wine-jar made after the Persian Wars.

Both sides of one of the silver ten-drachma pieces which may have been struck to celebrate Marathon. Notice the laurels.

to Sparta and back) had only the strength to gasp 'Rejoice, we have conquered!' before he collapsed and died of exhaustion. In his honour Marathon races were named. But how many people who have heard the story ever wonder why the runner killed himself? After all, what was the hurry? Since the Athenians had won, would an hour or two make much difference?

There was a very good reason. Though they had lost the battle, the Persians were still dangerous. Athens was only a few miles from the sea, and the Persian fleet had been seen to sail away in that direction. If the Persians arrived at Athens before the news reached the city, the people there would think that their army had been beaten, and might surrender. Besides, it was known that there were traitors in Athens, who might open one of the gates to the enemy. So the runner was not a fool. In fact, though, the army came marching back so quickly that it reached Athens before the Persian fleet. Outwitted, outfought and outmarched, the Persian general at last admitted defeat, and sailed away from Greece.

The Persians would try again. But the Great King had many things to do, and it was not until 480 B.C., ten years later, when Darius was dead and Xerxes reigned over the Persian Empire, that a new invasion was launched.

Meanwhile there were many people in Greece who expected that the Persians would return. In Athens a new leader called Themistocles believed that a strong fleet was even more important to his city than a strong army, and he persuaded the citizens to spend many of the coins you saw above in building war-galleys. In Sparta the warriors remembered that they had arrived too late for Marathon, and were determined that next time Sparta, not Athens, should earn most of the honour.

The great invasion

In 480 B.C. Xerxes brought together a vast army and a big fleet. He marched through Asia Minor. He was not going to rely on ferrying his men across the Aegean, but instead planned to make a bridge at the narrowest point, where the sea is only about a mile across. This is the Hellespont or Dardanelles, where Troy once stood. The map below shows you how Xerxes could then march his army all the way, while his fleet sailed along the coast by its side.

All went well for Xerxes. When he came to the Dardanelles the waves were rather rough at first, and there is a story that the king ordered his men to put the sea in chains and flog it until it behaved better. That is a story which the Greeks told. They would have thought it just the sort of madness which would come over a barbarian king who believed everything in the world must obey him. Whether or not the story is true, even the Greeks had to admit that Xerxes had first-class engineers. They built a strong bridge by anchoring a great number of boats side by side, and laid a road across them.

As Xerxes advanced, some Greek cities thought that it was hopeless to fight, and sent envoys to make friends with the Great King. Others thought that it was quite possible to stop the Persians, no matter how big their army was. The invaders would have to march through some passes between the mountains and the sea. You have only to remember Marathon to know what these Greeks were thinking.

The first pass is marked (1) on the map below. The Greeks occupied it, but then decided that it was too difficult to hold and left it.

The second pass is marked (2A). It is a place called Thermopylae ('Hot Gates' because of hot springs near the pass), and here a small force could keep back the biggest army in the world. Besides, at (2B) there was only a narrow strip of sea. The Greek galleys, like their soldiers, were fewer than those of Xerxes, and slower; but they were heavier, and had a much better chance in narrow waters like this. It was a very good position for the Greeks.

Now Sparta took the lead. King Leonidas, with 300 picked Spartans, the best warriors in all Greece, was entrusted with the defence of the pass. Other cities sent men to serve under Leonidas, so that he had an army of about 5,000 or more. With the galleys of Athens to protect his side next to the sea, and the mountains on the other side, Leonidas should be able to hold

Xerxes' invasion

Y   bridge built for Persian army
Z   canal dug for Persian fleet

the pass for a long time, while the other Greeks gathered together as big an army as they could.

Xerxes, knowing what a small army was in front of him, hurled masses of his soldiers against the defenders of the pass. But every Persian attack was hurled back again, with terrible losses. Even the Immortals, the king's own bodyguard, failed to shake the Spartans and their allies. Xerxes faced defeat.

Then Leonidas was betrayed.

There was a path through the mountains. A Greek who knew it went to Xerxes and sold his knowledge. A strong Persian force marched through the mountains, pushed aside the small Greek force which had been placed to watch that path, and came down behind Leonidas and his men.

The pass was lost, but there was time for Leonidas to withdraw his army. He sent most of his men back, to join the other Greeks who were preparing to fight the Persians. But he himself, with all his Spartans and 700 men from Thespiae, resolved to stay where they were. They knew that the position was now hopeless, and made ready to die. They washed themselves, and combed the long hair which warriors wore as a sort of cushion under their helmets, and awaited the Persian onslaught. When it was over, not a Greek remained alive on the battlefield.

Leonidas had been a hero. Had he also been a fool? You can argue about it for a long time. Do you think that he threw away the lives of 1,000 good soldiers who could have been very useful later? Or do you think that he gave an example to encourage the other Greeks and worry the Persians?

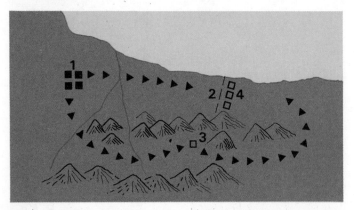

Thermopylae. 1 The Persian army. **2** Frontal attack at wall. **3** The flanking path through the mountains. **4** Spartans and allies.

However you judge Leonidas, one thing is certain. He had failed to hold the pass. The way was open now. The Persians surged forward. There was no chance of stopping them before the Isthmus of Corinth, marked (3) on the map on the previous page, which was less than five miles across. Athens lay between this and the Persians. Athens was doomed.

There had been a prophecy that when all seemed lost, Athens would be saved by her wooden walls. Most Athenians thought at first that this meant the Acropolis, the great rocky citadel which towered over the city, and which had once been fenced around by a wooden palisade; but others persuaded them that 'wooden walls' meant 'ships'. Crowding aboard ships, most of the people of Athens fled to the island of Salamis, only a few miles away.

At Salamis were gathered not only the people and ships of Athens, but also the war-galleys and generals of the other Greek city-states which were still fighting the Persians. Most of the Greek leaders wanted to retreat further, to the Isthmus of Corinth. Against this was one man, the Athenian leader Themistocles. He wanted to bring about a sea battle at Salamis. To understand why, we need to know a little about galley warfare.

Many people have the idea that a galley was a very simple sort of ship, where everything depended on brute force. Driven by oars, which were worked by slaves, the galley simply hit smack into the enemy with its ram. It was all very crude. That idea is completely wrong. Galleys were very cleverly designed and built, for they had to be both light and strong. It took great skill to sail and fight in a galley. With a clever captain and skilled oarsmen, a galley could almost turn in its own length, and there were all sorts of tricks for outwitting and sinking enemy galleys. There was too much skill in this for gangs of unwilling slaves to be used; neither the Greeks, nor the Romans, later, used galley-slaves, though some books and films may have made you think that they did.

Many of the galleys of Xerxes were Phoenician, and you will remember what good sailors the Phoenicians were. You saw how, off Thermopylae, narrow waters suited the Athenians best. Themistocles was cunning. He sent to Xerxes, pretending that he really wanted to change sides, and so tricked the Persian king into thinking that if he attacked with his ships at Salamis some of the Greek ships would join him and some would run away.

A Greek galley. Strengthening timbers met at the ram, and the prow is built up. In action the mast would be lowered on to the forked post set in the deck behind. The top bank of oars would be pivoted at the edge of the outrigger framework, the others through holes in the sides of the ship.

right: Close-up of prow.

far right: Close-up of stern.

So the Persian fleet sailed into a trap. From a nearby hill Xerxes watched while the Athenian captains, who knew the rocks, the bays, the concealed inlets where their galleys could hide in ambush, fell on the Persian galleys. The Persian fleet suffered such losses that it would not be able to face the Greek war-galleys again that year.

Now Xerxes realized his danger. There was nothing to prevent the Greeks from sailing to the Dardanelles and breaking the Persian bridge. Then Xerxes and his army would be cut off. Why did the Greeks not do this? They thought about it, and then had second thoughts. The Persian army was still very big, and it contained some very good soldiers. If they were trapped, they would know that they had to choose between death and victory. They would fight with desperate bravery and strength, and they were still so powerful that they might win after all. So the bridge remained.

Xerxes went, but he left part of his army behind, to hold those parts of Greece that he had conquered. The war did not end until the next year, 479 B.C. Then, at Plataea, after a very hard fight, the Persian army in Greece was destroyed. At Mycale the Persian fleet was beaten again. The great Persian attack on Greece had failed.

Though it happened so long ago, that war was a very important one for us. Even though we do not always realize it, we are constantly using ideas and even words that the Greeks invented. If Xerxes had won the war, he would probably have put an end to the free life of the city-states. Instead, the finest works of Greek civilization were to be made during the century after the defeat of the Persians.

The Delian League

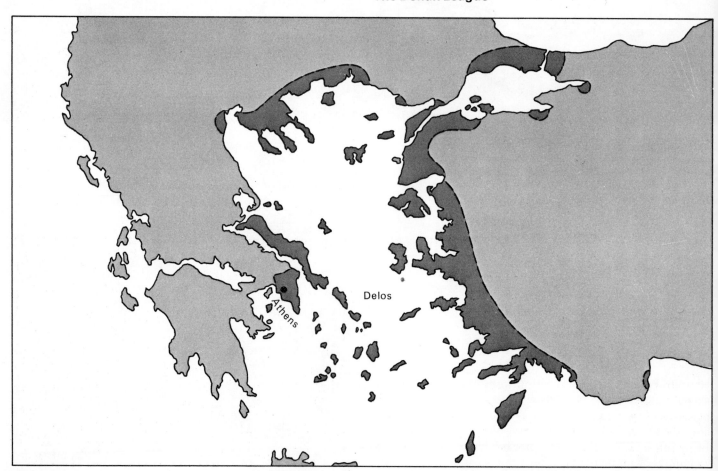

Athens the splendid

The Spartans were still renowned as the best warriors in Greece; they had fought heroically at both Thermopylae and Plataea. Yet it was the Athenians who had twice turned the tide of invasion, at Marathon and Salamis. Everybody knew this, and respected Athens because of it. Most of all, the Athenians knew it. Modesty was not a Greek virtue. The Athenians had a very high opinion of themselves, and began to think that they should be the leaders of the Greek city-states.

We know now that after 479 B.C. the Persians did not make any more attempts to conquer Greece, but how could the Greeks know that then? We can see the past, but they could not see the future, not even with the help of the oracle at Delphi. The king of Persia was still very strong. He could build a new fleet and try again. For fear of this, the Athenians suggested to many Greek cities on the islands and coasts of the Aegean Sea that they should all join forces. They should form an alliance, or league, so as to be ready to help each other as soon as the Persians once more sailed against the Greeks. Each city, according to its size and wealth, should provide war-galleys or money. Many cities joined, and they decided to keep the money and hold meetings on the sacred island of Delos. Therefore the league was called the Delian League. The map opposite shows you where the member cities of the Delian League were. It was a very good idea. As you know, the Greeks had been caught ill-prepared in 490 and 480 B.C., and had nearly been beaten. Now Athens was making sure that next time many of them would be ready.

However, the League soon began to change. The trouble was that Athens was so much stronger than the other members. The little cities especially were not able to afford to keep a war-galley or two, and paid money instead. Athens had the dockyards, the skilled ship-builders and the expert sailors, and Athens was very willing to keep a big navy, especially if the other cities of the League paid for it. So the Athenian fleet grew stronger and stronger. Then the treasure of the League, which had been kept at Delos, was thought to need a safer place. Delos was so small that some enemy might come and steal the money. So the money of the League was stored in a really safe place – Athens. Now Athens had most of the ships and all the funds of the League.

After a time some of the cities in the League began to wonder if all this was necessary. The Persians were not showing signs of being dangerous, and Athens was growing much too rich and powerful. So they decided to leave the League. A city that tried to do this soon discovered the truth. Athens would not let anyone leave the League, and Athens would not hesitate to send a fleet and an army to persuade a city to stay in.

In fact, what was called the Delian League was much more like an Athenian Empire. Athens was protecting her 'friends' from the Persians, but who could protect them against Athens? For many years there was no answer to that question.

Athens became very rich, very strong, the mistress of the Aegean Sea. Did she use her riches and strength well or badly? This you shall judge for yourself.

Athens and the sea

First, the Athenians, rebuilding the city after all the damage that the Persians had done, tried to make the city safe. They built very strong walls, strong enough to keep out the biggest enemy army. Even the strongest walls, however, cannot keep out hunger. The strongest city can be starved out. Athens had to be protected against this, too.

Though many of the citizens were still farmers, Athens now depended very much on trade. Much of the food for the city

The Black Sea corn route

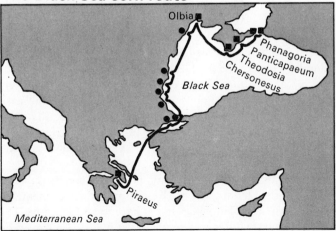

came from the shores of the Black Sea, where corn was grown by the citizens of Greek colonies. As long as the galleys of Athens ruled the sea, the corn supply was safe.

One difficulty remained. The city of Athens, though within sight of the sea, was not on the shore. It was about four miles from the harbour, which was at a place called Piraeus. This meant that there was the danger that an enemy could cut Athens off from the sea and from her ships. The answer was to build more walls, the famous 'Long Walls' as they were called, to protect the road and the port. This diagram shows how Athens was now linked to the sea. While her fleet ruled the sea, the walls of Athens would hold back any enemy on land.

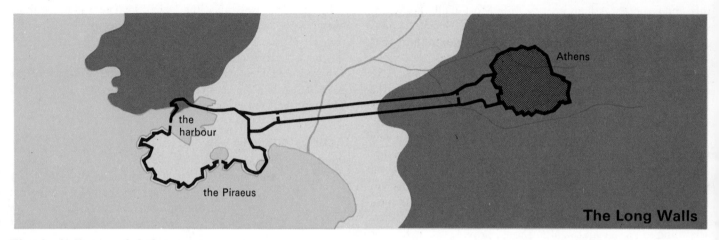

the harbour

the Piraeus

Athens

The Long Walls

The buildings of Athens

Inside the walls Athens was a very busy place. The Athenians spent their money less upon comfort and luxury in their homes than upon making their city beautiful. They spent most of their time out of doors, and they liked to have a beautiful city to look at. Besides, they were proud of their city. The finest work of all was done on the Acropolis, the citadel, the great rocky hill that had once been defended only by a wooden wall. Opposite is a picture of what the Athenians made of it. Even today, when they are ruined, these buildings are one of the most beautiful sights in the world.

Greek architecture looks easy. Purely as a piece of engineering, it is easy. But try to draw a Greek temple, and see how easy that is. Usually, when you have finished, the temple will be too high or too low. The pillars will be too thin or too fat. It just will not look right. In other words, you will have got the proportions wrong.

Talking about things like this is not much use. It is better to look at the buildings themselves, or at pictures of them. To see this style of building you do not have to go to Greece. The Greek style of building was so good that it has been copied by many people ever since, from the Romans to us. Do you know any buildings with something like **a** in front?

a

b

You can find churches, town halls, libraries, banks, big country houses, theatres, all with this sort of portico, as it is called. Even small houses often have doorways like **b**. We call this style of architecture 'classical', and it was specially popular in Europe only about 200 years ago. But you will hear about that when you come to it.

Athens; the hill of the Acropolis

The 'classical' front of the British Museum, started in 1823.

On the temples of the Acropolis, and most of all on the chief temple which was called the Parthenon, the men of Athens placed statues. Many of them were on a frieze which ran round the Parthenon just above the tops of the pillars. Some people think that the Greek temples are the most beautiful buildings ever to have been made, and in the same way there are many people who think that the Greeks were the finest sculptors who ever lived. You must try to judge for yourself. Many of the statues from the Parthenon are in the British Museum. It is best to look at the real statues, of course, because a photograph can only show you one side. Photographs are very useful, though. Compare this picture of Greek sculpture with pictures earlier in this book which showed the sculptures made by Egyptians and Assyrians. They are all very good, but do you agree that there is a life and grace in Greek statues that the others do not have?

Many Greek cities had fine buildings and statues, but none were as splendid as Athens.

below: Sculptures from the Parthenon.

right: The theatre of Dionysius, somewhat added to later, at Athens.

Greek theatres

Just below the Acropolis were the theatres. The Greeks were the first people to have plays. Every time you see a play, on the stage or on the screen, you are seeing something that the Greeks invented. 'Comedy' and 'tragedy' are Greek words. It all started as part of a religious service. At some services, songs and stories about the gods were sung and recited, rather like hymns and stories out of the Bible in one of our churches. People began to join in the chorus, or to give some of the replies if there was talking in the story. By the fifth century B.C., the time we are thinking about, the Greeks had gone on from this to have real plays, with actors and a chorus. Special places called theatres were built, so that the citizens could watch and hear the plays.

The picture shows you what a Greek theatre was like. You can see that, unlike ours, it was open to the sky. It was also much bigger. On the tiers of seats people could sit in thousands. The idea was not to have a show every night, but to hold a big festival each year on the feast of the god Dionysus, when everybody would be able to attend. There would be a number of plays at the festival and the plays would be judged in order of merit. All the citizens of Athens had to be able to see and

hear, and the theatres were so well made that this was possible.

When an Athenian went to the theatre he would go to see a new play, but he would usually know the story already. Greek poets took the old tales about gods and heroes which everybody knew, just as if modern play-wrights were to take their stories from the Bible or from the tales of King Arthur or King Alfred or Robin Hood. Then the Greek poet would try to show, in the play he wrote, what the old story meant, what it really was about.

Here is an example of the sort of tale which was used. After the fall of Troy, so the story went, King Agamemnon came home from the long war. While he had been away his wife, the queen, had fallen in love with someone else, so she murdered her husband and married the other man, making him king. Agamemnon's two children escaped and grew up. What should they do? It was the duty of every man to avenge the death of a murdered father, and if he failed to do this he would be punished by the gods. So the son of Agamemnon must kill Agamemnon's murderer. But that was his own mother. It was a terrible crime for a son to kill his mother, and if he did this he would be punished by the gods. What could the son and daughter of Agamemnon do? Whatever they did was bound to

In their plays the Greeks were interested in thoughts and feelings expressed in words, not in seeing realistic action. Actors wore masks, according to the sort of part they were playing. This is a tragic actor.

be wrong, bound to bring down on them the punishment of the gods. This is only part of the dark, savage, blood-spattered story of the kings of the House of Atreus, the sort of story that could easily be made into a 'horror' film nowadays.

However, the Greeks were not interested in horror for its own sake. They were much more interested in why people behaved as the queen had done; how the son and daughter would make up their minds and what they would do; and how the gods would finally judge what was right and what was wrong. Though the plays were often about violent and bloody deeds, violence and bloodshed were never seen on the stage. Murders and battles would be described by the actors, and the audience did not have to watch them. The Greeks thought that the theatre was a place where people should go to learn, to think, to feel sympathy with men and women who found themselves in such a terrible position as the children of Agamemnon. It was not a place for cheap thrills.

(If you think that this means the Greeks were soft, remember the Persian Wars.)

Watching tragedies was serious, and some light relief was needed. This was where comedies were put in. These usually made fun of the silly things that prominent people had done or said, or even of the silly things that all the citizens had done or said when they were meeting to talk about how the city should be run. The poets of Athens were brave men. Those who wrote tragedies were not afraid to question why the gods made life so hard for some people, and sometimes even to say that the gods themselves had been wrong. Those who wrote comedies were not afraid to tell their fellow-citizens a few home truths when they had been making fools of themselves.

Just as people still admire the buildings and statues which the Athenians made at this time, so they still admire their plays. New translations of the great Greek tragedies keep on being made, and they are often broadcast on the radio. Modern play-wrights like T. S. Eliot and Jean Anouilh have used the ideas in Greek plays, only bringing the settings up to date. The old Greek plays still have a lot to tell us about the way people think and feel.

Wise men

There are many books which people still read which were written at this time. Some of the most famous were written by Plato, and tell about Socrates. Most of the Athenians enjoyed

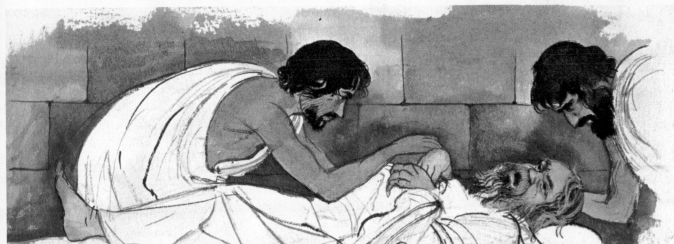

talking and asking questions, but nobody could ask questions like Socrates. Every time he met a man who was supposed to be very wise, Socrates would start asking questions, to see if he could learn anything from the wise man. These questions often seemed very simple and easy, but often they ended by showing how little the so-called wise man really knew.

Socrates was one of those Greeks who spent their time trying to find out the truth. These men were called 'philosophers', which means 'lovers of wisdom'. They kept on trying to find out. What is the world for? What are men for? How should people behave?

Socrates asked too many questions for his own safety. He made many enemies. Worse, some of the young men who had been his pupils turned out badly; they were very clever, but bad. They knew how to ask questions, but had come to believe that there were no real answers and that nothing was very important except themselves. Some of them betrayed Athens to her enemies. It makes a sad story. At last Socrates had to pay for what some of his pupils had done. He was put on trial. In spite of the fine speeches he made to show how mistaken were the charges against him, he was found guilty and condemned to die by most of the jury. He could have escaped, but refused, saying that he had never broken the laws of Athens and that he would always obey them. So the Athenian philosopher waited for death, and met it, as bravely as the Spartan king had done at Thermopylae.

Their books are one of the reasons why we have been spending more time on the Greeks than on the other great ancient

Though this picture of the death of Socrates is imaginary, the artist has copied Socrates' face from an ancient statue in the British Museum.

civilized peoples. It is not only that we are still using so many of their ideas. Another reason is that the Greeks are the first people we can really get to know, because they wrote so many books which tell us about the way they thought and felt and the things they did. The Greeks, for example, were the first people to write real history books. History is not just a list of facts and dates; history tries to show how and why people behave, make laws, win and lose battles, build and destroy. We know about the Persian Wars because Herodotus wrote about them, and tried to explain how and why things happened, and what was good and bad about both sides. In some ways, the Greek poets, philosophers and historians were all doing the same job. They were all trying to understand and to write about people.

The Athenians were not the only Greeks to make beautiful temples and statues or write great plays and books. Many other Greeks could do the same. Yet it was to Athens that most of the best artists and writers came. Athens was the place where people were most ready to listen and talk, to learn and argue, to try out new ideas. Athens was also rich, a good place for making a living; even artists and philosophers have to eat. So, by about 440 B.C., Athens was the real centre of everything that was going on in Greece. Some of the other city-states were not very pleased.

Sparta the grim

If the men of Athens were interested in everything, the men of Sparta were interested in only one thing. That thing was war.

A Spartan was trained for war from the moment he was born. Spartan babies who did not seem strong enough were put out to die. Spartan boys spent all their time running, jumping, carrying weapons and practising with them, living in rough camps in the wild mountains, learning to endure cold, hunger and pain. Sometimes their teachers would make them go out to steal their food from farms, to learn cunning. Even when he was a man, a Spartan had little freedom; he had to eat his meals and spend most of his time with the other warriors. Only the old men were able to live in their own homes.

There were no walls round the city. The Spartans thought that such protection would make them soft. There were no fine buildings, beautiful temples and theatres. The Spartans thought that a true warrior should have no interest in such things. There was hardly any trade, and Spartan money was made of heavy lumps of iron, hard to carry about. The Spartans thought that meeting foreigners might give them new ideas, and they did not trust new ideas. Buying foreign goods would make them fond of luxury. Becoming rich would make them selfish.

The Spartans did not even talk much; soldiers do not chatter. They did not ask questions and argue; soldiers give orders and carry out orders.

Anyway, there was nothing to ask questions about. Nothing in Sparta was ever changed. The Spartans were determined to carry on their strict, orderly life, and were always prepared to defend it against anyone who tried to upset things.

This may seem strange, after what you have heard about the Greeks already. But there was a very good reason why the Spartans were so different. That reason was the Helots. The Helots were the people who had lived in Sparta before the Spartans came. The Spartans had conquered them, and made them do all the hard work. Spartans and Helots never mixed, never inter-married. The Helots were a subject people, but they were not ordinary slaves, the sort of slaves who could be bought and sold. Helots were bound to certain jobs, bound to work on certain farms. When a Spartan was given a farm, he was given the Helots to work on it; whoever became master, the Helots went on working. They were kept down by the Spartans, treated as if they were not much better than beasts. Of course they hated the Spartans, and there were perhaps ten times as many Helots as Spartans. It was this ever-present danger which made the Spartans what they were.

Spartan women were nearly as tough as Spartan men. When they were girls, they had a training which was only a little less hard than that of the men; they too had to run and jump, to endure cold and hardship. Their job was not to be warriors, but to be the wives and mothers of warriors. When a Spartan woman said goodbye to her husband or son as he marched away to war, she did not weep. She handed him his heavy round shield and said to him: 'Come back with it or on it.'

They were a grim set of people, these Spartans. They were not very much like most of the other Greeks. The other Greeks, however, had a great respect for the Spartans, and this was not only because the Spartans were so good at fighting. The main reason was that the Spartans lived up to their beliefs, hard though these beliefs were. It was respect, not fear. The Spartans were not like that other warlike people you know about, the Assyrians. They were not interested in conquering other cities in order to make an empire, and they did not take pleasure in cruelty. Even though they were such great warriors, the Spartans did not look for trouble. They usually had to be brought into a war by the actions of some other city.

The downfall of Athens

Sooner or later a war was almost bound to happen. Athens and Sparta were opposite to each other in almost everything. Meanwhile Athens kept on growing richer and stronger, and interfered more and more with the business of other city-states. The other Greek cities were annoyed and rather frightened of Athens, and looked to Sparta to protect them. Finally, in 431 B.C. the great war started.

The leader of Athens was Pericles, the man who for years had guided his fellow-citizens in making the city so beautiful and powerful. He had foreseen this war for a long time, and he knew how to win it. He knew that the soldiers of Athens were no match for the soldiers of Sparta in an ordinary battle, phalanx against phalanx, but they could easily beat back the Spartans from the walls of Athens and the Long Walls. Therefore Pericles brought all the people from the countryside around Athens into the city. It was crowded, but the ships could bring in plenty of food for everybody. The Spartans could march all over the countryside, but they could not harm Athens itself.

There was one thing that Pericles had forgotten. Too many people were crowded within the walls. When people have to live like that, they find it harder to keep clean and healthy. If an illness breaks out, it can spread very quickly. Illness did break out. Athens was struck by a plague, a dreadful disease which swept away people in their hundreds. Among those who died was Pericles himself.

Pericles had never been a king, or a tyrant, or anything like that. He was just an ordinary citizen, like all the other citizens of Athens. He was so wise and clever, and so often right that the other citizens got into the habit of taking his advice and often electing him as their general in war. Now he was dead. Would the Athenians be able to find other leaders as good as Pericles?

Some men are able to make speeches and persuade other people to follow them. Such men, who are called demagogues, may be wise and good; but they may not. A man can be a good speaker without being good at much else. There was at this time in Athens a man called Cleon, and he was a demagogue. Though he was neither wise nor good, he was able to make the Athenians follow him. At first he was very lucky. He caught a force of Spartans on an island and took them prisoner; Spartans never surrendered – but these Spartans had surrendered to Cleon.

By now there were men on both sides who wanted to make peace. Neither Athens nor Sparta looked like ever being able to beat the other. Yet Cleon dragged on the war for three more years. Finally, after he was killed in a lost battle, a treaty was made – and almost immediately broken.

The expedition to Syracuse

It was Athens which caused trouble again, restless, ambitious, brilliant Athens, led now by a restless, ambitious, brilliant young man called Alcibiades. Athens could not resist the temptation to meddle in other people's business, and this led her to attack the city of Syracuse, in far-away Sicily. Syracuse was rich and strong, and Athens would have to send a very big fleet and army to fight more than 700 miles across the sea. But Athens thought that she could do anything. Most of the citizens felt sure that in a few months they would own a fine new empire in Sicily. Taking no notice of those citizens who argued for peace, who said that it was dangerous, that it was wrong, and that Athens had no use for an empire, the Athenians sent out the mightiest fleet and army that any Greek city had ever possessed.

You know the saying, 'Pride goes before a fall.' There is another expression, 'Tempting providence.' Both of these sayings are part of a very old idea, an idea that most peoples seem to have known. Certainly the Greeks knew it. They believed that a man, or a city, could become too proud. The sort of pride that makes people believe that they are always right and always bound to get whatever they want, that they must always win, had a special name in Greece. It was called 'hubris'. People who had hubris forgot that they were not gods. They forgot that no man can be sure of the future. They forgot that famous saying of a great Athenian: 'Call no man happy till he dies.' This sort of pride, this hubris, made the gods angry, and disaster came.

Of that proud fleet and army which sailed away from the Piraeus to conquer Syracuse, hardly a ship or a man came back. Held before the walls of Syracuse, the Athenians would not believe that they could not take the city. They stayed there, month after month, certain that the next attack was bound to succeed. Attack after attack failed, but still the Athenians would not give up and go home. They stayed too long. Their enemies gathered. The Athenian ships were trapped in a bay

The route of the Athenian expedition to Syracuse.

The Athenian fleet on its way to Syracuse.

and wiped out. The army could not sail away now. It tried to march to another part of Sicily, but was cut off. Many men were killed and the rest were taken prisoner. The prisoners were herded into some stone quarries, with no shelter from heat or cold, and little food or water. Here they were kept until many of them died of their sufferings, and for a long time the corpses of the dead were left piled up beside the living. After eight months the survivors were taken out and sold as slaves.

The disaster was terrible, and from it you can see that the Greeks could be merciless, even to Greeks like themselves. The Athenians were the sufferers this time, but they could be just as hard. Only three years before the disaster at Syracuse the Athenians had conquered the little island of Melos; they had killed all the men, and sold all the women and children as slaves. Though they did not love cruelty, the Greeks could be savage when they were angry.

The last years of the war

Athens had suffered a terrible blow, the sort of blow that could have ended the war. But the Spartans were slow, and the Athenians worked hard. In the treasury of Athens was a great sum of money which had been put aside long ago, to be used only when the city was in such danger that only this treasure could save it. Now the danger had come, and the treasure was used. Within a year war-galleys of Athens were at sea once more, sweeping the Aegean and protecting the corn-ships. Athens fought on. To the surprise of the Spartans, Athens seemed soon to be as strong as ever.

Though they were brave and clever, the people of Athens could sometimes be foolish. Sometimes, as you have seen, they chose bad leaders or followed bad advice. They also had a habit of turning on generals who had led them to victory. Alcibiades, for example, who might have saved the army and fleet at Syracuse, was driven away from Athens and helped the Spartans for a time. Then Athens took him back, and he won victories at sea and was treated like a saviour. Then, through no fault of his own, he lost some galleys, and immediately the Athenians turned on him and drove him once more into exile. The very next year a group of Athenian admirals won a great victory, but a storm blew after the battle and many Athenian ships were sunk with all their men. When the admirals came back to Athens they were blamed for not having rescued the shipwrecked men, put on trial and condemned to death.

A quarry of Syracuse, with captured Greeks.

Socrates alone protested that this was unjust and illegal. The admirals were all executed. Soon afterwards the Athenians realized what wrong they had done, when it was too late.

Meanwhile the Spartans seemed to have no means of beating the Athenians. The Spartans even tried to get the Persians to help them against Athens. Though the Persians were not such fools as to want to see any Greek state become too strong, they kept the Spartans going by giving them money. At last the Spartans, who usually had more brawn than brains, found a clever leader, a man called Lysander.

Lysander knew that in an ordinary battle he could never beat the galleys of Athens, so he must try some other way. He took his fleet to the Dardanelles. Look at the map on page 71, and you will see what this meant. The corn-ships had to pass through the narrow straits of the Dardanelles, and Lysander could attack them. This was a threat to the life-line of Athens. At once the Athenian fleet came after him. Lysander took shelter in the harbour of Lampsacus, which he had just captured, where the Athenians could not attack him. He did not dare to come out and fight. The Athenians took their galleys to the other side of the straits, pulled them on to the beach at a place called Aegospotami (Greek for 'Goat River'), and camped for the night. Next morning they sailed back to challenge the Spartan fleet. Lysander drew up his ships in order of battle, but did not leave the harbour. Everybody could see that he did not dare to fight the Athenians. This happened for four days. Each day the Athenians became more certain that the Spartan fleet was afraid to fight. This was exactly what Lysander wanted them to think. The Athenians were falling into a trap.

By chance, Alcibiades was living in exile nearby. Though he had been badly treated by his fellow-citizens, he still loved his city. He could not bear to think of what was going to happen. He rode into the Athenian camp, went to the Athenian admirals, and warned them that Lysander was a clever and bold admiral and that the Athenians should beware. His words were wasted. The Athenian admirals called him a traitor and chased him away. Alcibiades had been right, though. The fifth evening, when the Athenian fleet had returned from challenging the Spartans, more sure than ever that they were afraid to face the fleet of Athens, the Spartans suddenly came out. It was less than two miles to the Athenian camp, and the Spartans were there before the Athenians could get their galleys afloat

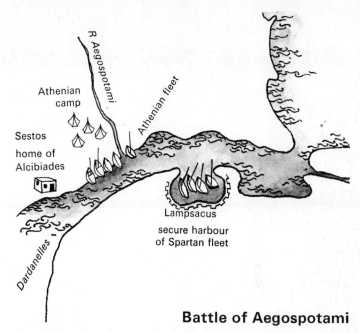

Battle of Aegospotami

The long left hook : Epaminondas' winning tactic when defeating Sparta at the battle of Leuctra. To ensure a decisive majority on his left, the Theban's centre and right must have been very weak indeed.

and into battle order. Nine Athenian galleys escaped. For the rest, it was not a battle but a massacre. It has been said that in one hour Lysander ended a war which had lasted for twenty-seven years. Lysander killed all his prisoners and sailed for Athens.

Without a fleet, without corn, Athens soon began to starve, and asked for peace. Some of the other Greeks wished for revenge, and would have treated Athens as Athens had treated Melos. Sparta, in her hour of victory, was more generous. The Spartans remembered what all the Greeks had owed to Athens eighty years before, at the time of the Persian Wars, and refused to allow such a city to be destroyed. Athens was given peace, but had to pull down the Long Walls and keep only twelve war-galleys, and had to promise never to go against the wishes of Sparta.

Athens was still a great city, and was still the centre for the best artists and writers and speakers in Greece, but never again threatened to rule over the other Greek cities.

The downfall of Sparta

Now Sparta was the chief city of Greece, without a rival. Athens had lost the great war, and the Spartans were, as always, the best fighters in Greece. Yet that was not the reason why they had defeated the Athenians. As you have seen, the Spartans had won because the Athenians had made too many mistakes and because the Spartans found a clever leader.

In 371 B.C. the Spartans went to war against the men of Thebes. The two armies faced each other. Though there had been in other wars, as you know, defeats and disasters for Sparta, there had never once been a Spartan defeat in an ordinary pitched battle, phalanx against phalanx. This was going to be such a straightforward battle, and so the Spartans had every reason to think that they would win.

They drew up their army in the way Greek armies always were drawn up. The diagram on this page shows you how it was done, in three solid phalanxes. The phalanxes were roughly the same size, but the Spartans placed their very best soldiers on the right. No other Greek phalanx could be expected to stand up to the terrible strength of a Spartan right.

The Theban general, Epaminondas, now had a very difficult problem to solve. His soldiers were good, but they were not as good as the famous Spartans. He did not have enough of them to crush the Spartans by sheer weight of numbers. The battle was about to be fought on an open plain, so that there could be no surprises or ambushes. There were no new weapons which would astonish and shatter the enemy. It looked as though the Thebans were bound to be beaten.

Yet there was a way to win, and quite a simple way. Epaminondas found it.

The first part of the answer to the problem was this. Epaminondas made his left so big that it would be able to smash even the Spartan right by sheer weight. A fight between two phalanxes was simply a push-of-war. Unless the soldiers on one side ran away, the biggest and heaviest would win. Epaminondas made sure that his left would destroy the Spartan right.

All very well, you may say, but what would be happening on the rest of the battlefield, where the Thebans would be much weaker than the Spartans? Epaminondas had the answer to this, too. He would place his centre so far back that, by the time the Spartan centre began to hurt it, the Theban left would have finished with the Spartan right and would be able to turn on the Spartan centre. In the same way, the Theban right could be still weaker, and kept still farther back. So the two armies were arranged as the next diagram shows.

That was how 10,000 of the unbeatable Spartans were beaten by only 6,000 Thebans, at the battle of Leuctra. Simple, isn't it?

Nearly all brilliant ideas look simple – once they have been explained. After all, could anything be much simpler than a wheel? Yet, though wheels were known from the very beginnings of Mesopotamian civilization, great civilizations arose in America which never discovered the idea. The man who

The normal arrangement of a phalanx : three roughly
equal blocks of men.

discovered that simple thing, the wheel, was a genius. So was
Epaminondas.

   After the Spartans had been beaten in this and other battles
by Epaminondas, they lost their old power. There was now no
longer any city-state which the others admitted to be the
strongest. Thebes could not take the place of Sparta, because
it was only the genius of Epaminondas, not the strength of
Thebes, that had brought victory. It looked as though, now
that Athens and Sparta had in turn been taught their lesson,
the little states of the Greeks could go on with their free life.

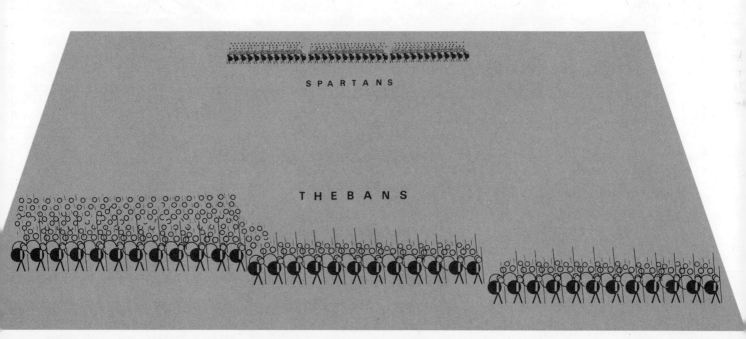

SPARTANS

THEBANS

Alexander

About this time there was, to the north of Greece, a poor, rough kingdom called Macedon. The people were mostly shepherds, for the land was too barren for good farming. The king was a man named Philip, and he was not satisfied with being king of such a poor and backward land. He knew that his people were very tough, and would make good soldiers if he could train them. Philip had once known Epaminondas, and he trained his men carefully to use long spears and to carry out his orders. Philip also saw that the Greek city-states were so fond of quarrelling among themselves that he could play them off against one another – and the Greeks would never suspect a poor ignorant Macedonian of being clever enough to do anything like that.

Philip's plans worked. By the time the Greek cities saw what he was doing, it was too late. Those which fought were beaten by the fine new Macedonian army. Philip was master of Greece. He did not call himself King of Greece, because he knew that the Greeks would take this as a great insult and would never be able to forget or forgive it. He simply became the 'protector' of the Greek cities. He persuaded them to form a league in order to invade the Persian Empire, and had himself appointed general of all the soldiers of all the Greek cities. (You may remember that something rather like this had happened before in Greece.) Before he could attack the Persians, Philip was murdered. There is still a mystery about who was behind the murder.

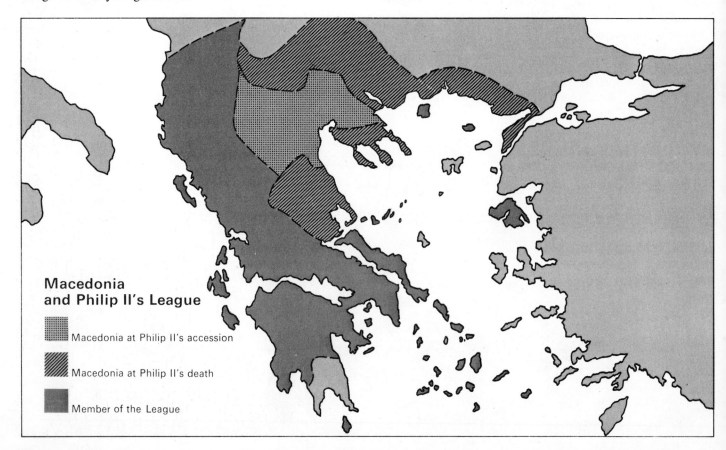

Macedonia and Philip II's League

Macedonia at Philip II's accession

Macedonia at Philip II's death

Member of the League

Alexander invades the Persian Empire.

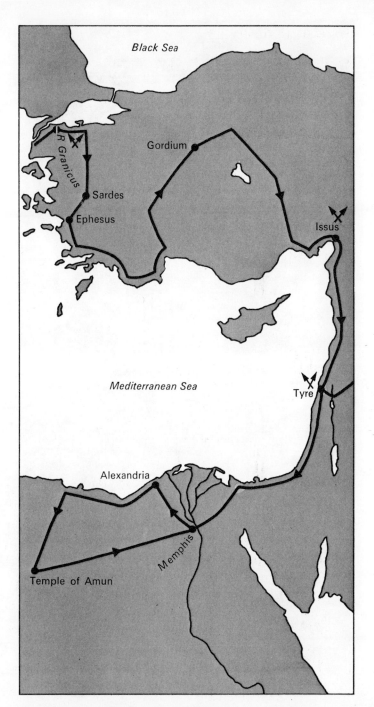

Philip's son, Alexander, was only twenty. This was a wonderful chance for all Philip's enemies. With such a boy on the throne, Macedon would soon be put in its place.

What happened was amazing. This young man took command of the Macedonian army, gave orders to his father's generals as if he had been doing it for years, and fell on his enemies. He was quick and he never made a mistake. Thebes, which had caused most trouble, was almost completely destroyed, and the people were sold as slaves. Within a few months Alexander had shown that he was well able to begin where his father had ended. Then, as leader of the Greek cities and King of Macedon, he led his army against Persia.

From this moment onwards, Alexander's career is just one victory after another. He always won, so that the story almost becomes monotonous. This map shows you some of the things he did in the first three years of his march into the Persian Empire.

By the middle of the year 331 B.C. he had defeated two great Persian armies, the second of them led by the Persian king himself. He had become master of Asia Minor and Syria. He had taken the island city of Tyre after a tremendous siege, during which he had even built out the land until it reached the island, and Tyre was an island no longer. He had been welcomed by the Egyptians, who chose him instead of the Persian to be their king and thought that he was the son of their great god Amun. On some of his coins, like the one on the next page, Alexander was shown with ram's horns, the sign of Amun, in his hair.

Alexander, decorated with the Horns of Amun, as shown on a coin of Lysimachus, one of his generals, who inherited a slice of Alexander's empire.

All this was only the beginning. Now he plunged into the middle of the Persian Empire. King Darius III of Persia raised the biggest army he could, and with this vast host he met Alexander between Arbela and Gaugamela. Alexander won, and Darius fled. Alexander marched into Mesopotamia, and all the great cities opened their gates to him, and took him as their king. Poor Darius, hunted by Alexander's soldiers, was at last murdered by some of his own men, and Alexander sat on his throne. He was now the lord of all the old civilized lands of the Middle East, as well as being King of Macedon and leader of the Greeks.

The Persians treated Alexander as they had treated all their other kings. They fell down before him, and made him feel almost as if he were a god. He liked it. His old friends in his army, Macedonians and Greeks, found that they could not

Alexander marched from endless plains to endless mountains this view shows the country northwards from Ecbatana, today called Hamadan, just as Persia is now called Iran.

Gaugamela: the decisive moment in the story of a great general, as imagined by a Roman mosaic artist 200 years later. In fact, Alexander and Darius did not meet face to face.

talk to him as they used to. They began to grumble that Alexander was beginning to turn into a Persian himself. One night this suddenly flared up. Alexander had an old friend called Cleitus; they had been boys together, and Cleitus had saved Alexander's life in their first battle against the Persians. They quarrelled, and in his rage Alexander picked up a spear and killed his friend. They were probably both very drunk at the time, but that is a poor excuse. When he saw what he had done, Alexander shut himself up for days, weeping and lamenting for the friend he had killed. Some of his men were as worried by this as by the murder itself. It all showed that Alexander was losing control of himself. He was paying the price for his victories.

As time went on, Alexander began to be suspicious. He knew that some of his generals did not like the way he was behaving, and he was afraid that some of them were plotting against him. He had some executed, some murdered.

Still he was popular with most of the soldiers, for he was still a great leader of an army in war. He did not stay for long in the palaces of the Persian kings, but set off again, to conquer more.

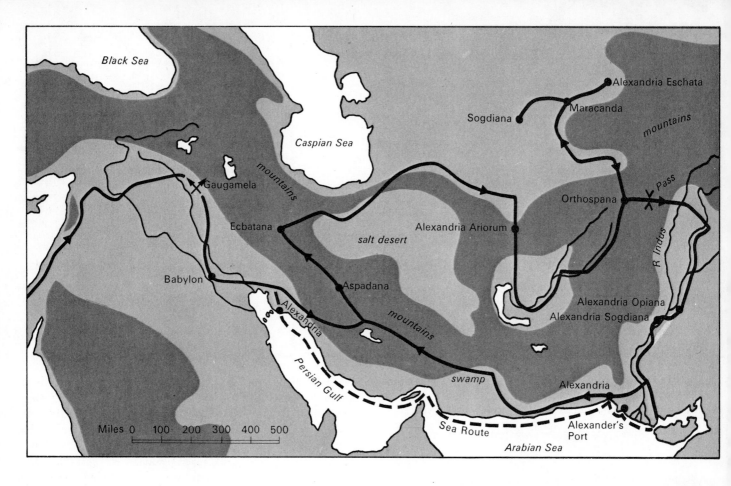

Map labels:
Black Sea
Caspian Sea
Sogdiana
Alexandria Eschata
Maracanda
mountains
Gaugamela
mountains
Ecbatana
salt desert
Alexandria Ariorum
Orthospana
Pass
R Indus
Babylon
Aspadana
Alexandria
mountains
Alexandria Opiana
Alexandria Sogdiana
Persian Gulf
swamp
Alexandria
Miles 0 100 200 300 400 500
Sea Route
Alexander's Port
Arabian Sea

The final conquest of Persia, and the great colonizing,
fact-finding, fighting and ultimately fatal march made by
Alexander; one of the greatest military expeditions
ever mounted.

Nobody quite seemed to know where the Persian Empire
ended, where the frontier exactly was. Alexander wanted to
find out. He marched all round and beyond his frontiers, for
hundreds and thousands of miles. He marched through the
hills and mountains to the limitless plains, where the wild
nomads lived with their herds. Wherever he went, he founded
new towns and named them after himself. In each new town
he left some soldiers who had to settle there and hold the place.
Then he marched on again, fighting all who tried to stop him.

Weary at last of the barren, endless plains, he turned south.
Now he came to the high mountains, those mountains which
are sometimes known as 'the Roof of the World', the Hima-
layas. Still he pushed on, through dark passes and by dizzy
heights. Wherever he went, he beat the people who fought

him, from the galloping horsemen of the wide plains to the savage tribesmen who lurked among the mountains. He not only beat them, but he usually won their respect and even friendship. Afghans still tell stories about the deeds of Iskander, as they call him, and some of them who have blue eyes claim to be descended from the Macedonian soldiers he left in the new towns among the mountains.

Beyond the mountains Alexander found a rich plain, and was among civilized people once more. But this was a civilization that he had not met before. He had reached India. He still had to fight. The Indian King Porus came against Alexander with a terrifying new weapon – huge beasts which could smash down anything in their path. Even these, the elephants, could not stop Alexander. He beat Porus, took him prisoner, and made a friend of him.

Now Alexander prepared to go on, into the centre of India, to conquer new peoples and found new towns. But he was stopped. His soldiers could endure no more. They refused to go any further, and Alexander had to promise to lead them back to Persia.

Even now he had to do something new. He would not return by the way he had already travelled. So he marched back through new country, which turned out to be mostly desert, where many of his men died of thirst and hunger and weariness. Some of the army he had sent back by sea, in ships that they had built in India. They, too, suffered badly from thirst and hunger.

Soon after he had returned to Mesopotamia, in the great and ancient city of Babylon, Alexander fell ill and died. He was only 32, but he had done enough to wear out the strength of a hundred men, and now even he was worn out.

The world has seen many great conquerors, but none so great as Alexander. Next to the men who began the world's great religions, Alexander is probably the most famous man in history.

A pass in Afghanistan.

After Alexander

What had Alexander been trying to do?

Nobody really knows the answer. Perhaps he started because the plan had already been made by his father, and went on because there was no particular reason why he should stop. Perhaps he really did think that he could rule the whole world. He did not know how big the world was. Some people think that he was most of all an explorer, always wanting to know what lay beyond the horizon. Some people think that he wanted to teach all the nations in his empire to live peacefully together in the most civilized way they could. He himself had been brought up to admire the civilization of the Greeks, and had been taught by one of the most famous of all the Greek philosophers, Aristotle. He may have wished that everybody in the world could learn from the Greeks.

People will always argue about Alexander and what he was trying to do, and they may all be right. It is just possible that he may have wanted to do everything – to fight, to explore, to rule the world, to teach everyone what the Greeks had to give to the world. We shall never know for certain.

What did Alexander succeed in doing?

You know already what he did. He won all his battles, caused thousands of people to be killed, founded dozens of towns, and made himself the ruler of a vast empire. That is what he did in his short life.

But how long did it last?

Almost at once, the great empire fell apart. Alexander's generals carved it up, and eventually the two main pieces of it were a new Egyptian kingdom ruled by General Ptolemy, and a great kingdom covering most of the rest of the old Persian Empire ruled by General Seleucus. The old homes of civilization were still at the hearts of two great kingdoms, but the new kings were Macedonian-Greek. There were also many Greeks in the new towns of the Middle East, and in many of the old cities too. Alexander had certainly spread the Greeks and their influence. We can see this from the map.

The Successor States, the main kingdoms which Alexander's generals carved out of his empire.

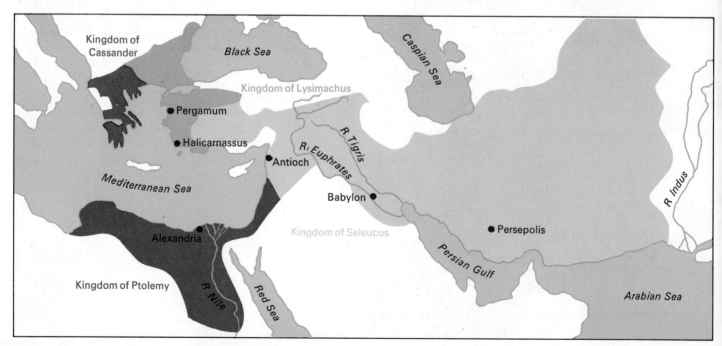

The Hellenistic Age

To the Greeks themselves Alexander may have done something more important. Now that they lived in great kingdoms, the Greeks did not feel free. Some of them tried to pretend that their city-states in Greece were still free, but everybody really knew that no polis could be truly independent among all the big kingdoms and empires. Whatever a citizen thought or said or did, the last word would always be spoken by some powerful king. Greeks could never again feel as free as they had before the Macedonians came.

Have you ever heard anyone described as being cynical? Or stoical? Or sceptical? Or epicurean? These are all words that we still use when we want to say that people are behaving in a certain way. They are all Greek, and they are the names of the new ideas which new philosophers invented, to help people to make the most of their lives even if they were no longer the free citizens of free city-states.

The Greeks were still a very clever race, and they did some very clever things. Many of the cleverest lived in Egypt, in the city of Alexandria which Alexander had built and where Ptolemy and his descendants ruled as kings. Here there was a great library, where scholars could use the finest collection of books in the world. Into the harbour of Alexandria ships from all over the Mediterranean Sea were guided by a towering lighthouse, so magnificent that it was included as one of the Seven Wonders of the World. These scholars of Alexandria were often amazingly clever. One of them, called Eratosthenes, measured the length of shadows cast by the sun at different places in Egypt, and from this was able to work out the size of the world. Although we are not quite certain of the measurements he was using, it seems likely that he got very near the truth. There was another man, called Hero, who invented a steam engine, though no use was made of it. Some of these devices are explained on the next double page. The Greeks were at least as intelligent as ever.

They knew that there was something else needed, besides cleverness, and that the great days of Marathon and Thermopylae had gone for ever. That is why we call the Greeks after Alexander 'Hellenistic'. The Greeks' own name for themselves was 'Hellenes', and anything belonging to them should be called 'Hellenic'. 'Hellenistic' means 'Like, but not quite, Greek'. It is the difference between saying a thing is real, and saying that it is realistic. A thing that is realistic is a good

The pharos, or great lighthouse, of Alexandria.

93

One of Hero of Alexandria's ingenious toys.
When the apple, A, was lifted, Hercules let fly his arrow into the dragon's eye. Water compressed air, released from below, made the dragon hiss.

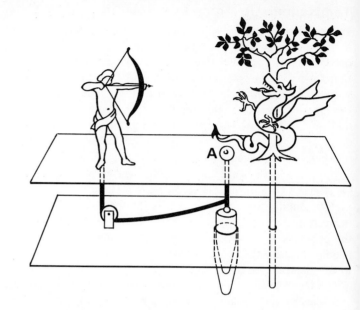

Hero's Device for Opening Temple Doors
When the fire was lit, it heated the air in the box. The hot air expanded and forced water from the sphere, up the pipe, into the bucket.

As the bucket filled, it became heavier than the weight which had been balancing it, and pulled downwards on the ropes. The ropes turned the pillars, which opened the temple doors. When the fire was put out, the air in the box cooled and shrank, the water was sucked back from the bucket, the ropes were pulled in the opposite direction and the doors closed.

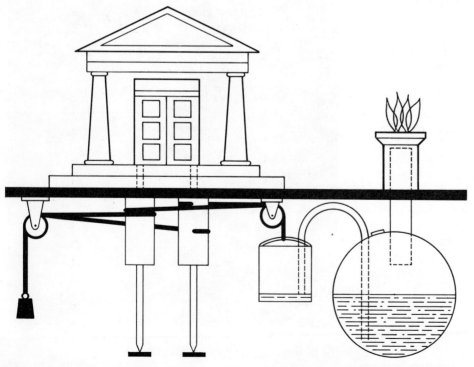

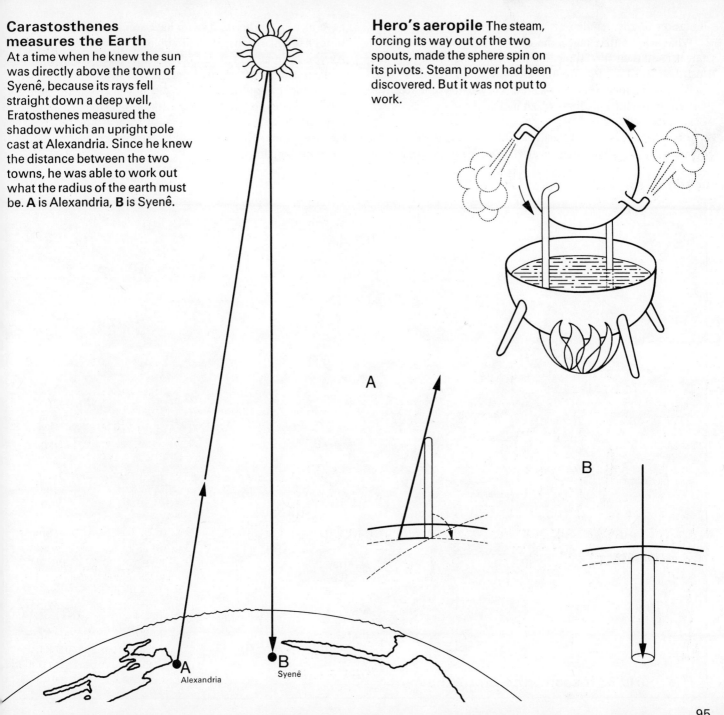

Carastosthenes measures the Earth
At a time when he knew the sun was directly above the town of Syenê, because its rays fell straight down a deep well, Eratosthenes measured the shadow which an upright pole cast at Alexandria. Since he knew the distance between the two towns, he was able to work out what the radius of the earth must be. **A** is Alexandria, **B** is Syenê.

Hero's aeropile
The steam, forcing its way out of the two spouts, made the sphere spin on its pivots. Steam power had been discovered. But it was not put to work.

A

B

A
Alexandria

B
Syenê

imitation of the genuine article, but it is not the real thing.

What was it that made the difference between these new Greeks and their forefathers? Many of them felt that they had lost their freedom, for freedom was something that they could only have in their little city-states. They could not feel free citizens in the big kingdoms which had arisen after Alexander's conquests.

It had been this idea of freedom which had made the Greeks different from all the other great civilized peoples whom you have met in this book. As you have seen, the men of the city-states had done many fine and noble things with their freedom. As you have also seen, they had sometimes been foolish and wicked. The city-states had one weakness, however, which at last brought them down. They did not discover any way for free city-states to live together without quarrelling. So it happened that, although they managed to beat off the Persians, the time came when they had to give place to the big and powerful kingdoms.

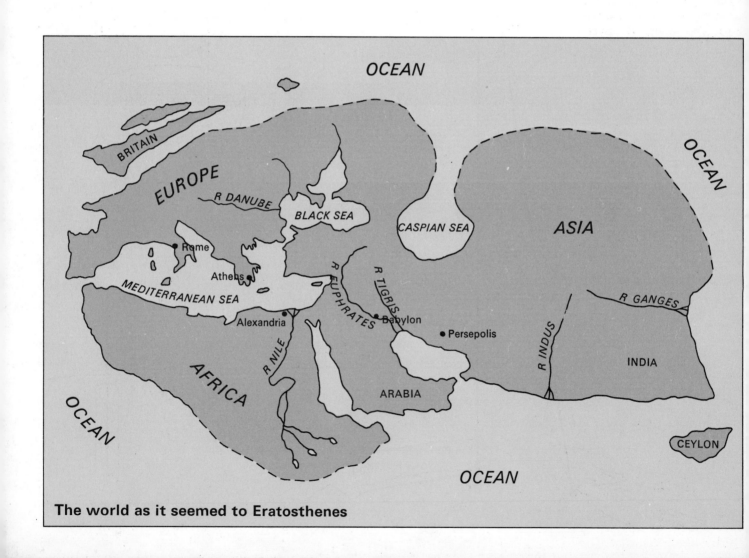

The world as it seemed to Eratosthenes